Dream
of the Goddess

Discovering the Divine While You Sleep

Scarlett Ross

NEW PAGE BOOKS
A division of The Career Press, Inc.
Franklin Lakes, NJ

DREAMS OF THE GODDESS
EDITED AND TYPESET BY KRISTEN MOHN
Cover design by Cheryl Cohan Finbow
Printed in the U.S.A. by Book-mart Press
Interior artwork by John Ross
Clipart ©2002 www.ArtToday.com

To order this title, please call toll-free 1-800-CAREER-1 (NJ and Canada: 201-848-0310) to order using VISA or MasterCard, or for further information on books from Career Press.

The Career Press, Inc., 3 Tice Road, PO Box 687,
Franklin Lakes, NJ 07417
www.careerpress.com
www.newpagebooks.com

Library of Congress Cataloging-in-Publication Data

Ross, Scarlett.
    Dreams of the goddess : discovering the divine while you sleep / Scarlett Ross.
        p. cm.
    Includes bibliographical references and index.
    ISBN 1-56414-603-0 (pbk.)
        1. Dreams. 2. Dream interpretation. 3. Goddess religion. I. Title.

BF1091 .R76 2002
135'.3—dc21

2002022230

Dedication

To my mother—for teaching me to dream.

To my husband—for helping my dreams come true.

To my son—for being a dream every day.

To Trish—for helping me become the person I should be.

To the IHOP crew—Julie, Jan, Dawn, Edgar, Debbie, Chris, Cheryl, Shannon—thanks for the fries, guys!

To Twilight—a real dreamer.

To the dreamers who opened up their dreams—Ron, Ricky, K'La, and Sarsen.

To the Goddess, who guided my pen along every page and blessed me in this endeavor for discovery.

Contents

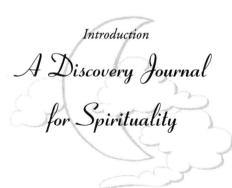

Introduction

A Discovery Journal
for Spirituality

Dreams are the key to seeing the spirit of humankind and into the heart of the Goddess. These nightly adventures are wonderful tools for personal growth, psychological health, spiritual awareness, and connecting and communicating with the Goddess. Unfortunately, we're not all locksmiths, and we forget our keys from time to time! (The term *goddess* is used because it is the feminine divine energy that this book brings into the dream realm. Other forms of divinity, whether they are male, animal, astral, or celestial, can be substituted wherever the name of the Goddess appears.)

Your dreams continue to grow and change as your world changes around you. Nonetheless, many modern dream books are still filled with images and interpretive values from a century ago. *Dreams of the Goddess* brings your dreaming into the 21st century by taking into account the new symbols that have come into today's world, multi-cultural influences, and the role that Spirit can (and should) play in your dreams.

If you are a new dreamer, you might find that friends, family, or coworkers scoff at the value of dream Craft. In the pages of this book, however, you will find no such denials (and

perhaps some ideas for finding supportive dreamers around you). Instead of dismissing your slumbering visions, *Dreams of the Goddess* advocates finding meaning, sustenance, encouragement, faith, advice, motivation, and solace in your dreams through active participation and interpretation. As you walk through the history and science of dreaming to the practice of modern dreams, this book and its journal exercises will illustrate the connection between the Goddess and you in the dreamscape. The chapters and exercises will support the connection between you and your Goddess so it grows stronger and more secure.

The concept that the Goddess can be part of dreams may seem foreign to some, but from an historical viewpoint, the Sacred Powers and Spirits have always had an honorable place in dreaming. Some of the African diaspora religious traditions hear the voice of their Ancestors in the changing scenery of dreams. Native religions in the United States treat dreams as the sacred voice of the gods and encourage the sharing of dreams. Jewish tradition considers dream interpretation to be one of the few acceptable forms of divination. All of these paths, and many others, recognize that the voices and images in the night are the echoes of the Divine speaking to us. This book will help you rediscover that echo, and then to find your own voice.

To accomplish that goal, *Dreams of the Goddess* includes a a section for journaling in each chapter. The journal space provided should serve as a starting point for your ideas and should not restrict you in any way. I strongly encourage you to be persistent and patient in undertaking the activities. The journal entries provide you with a process for self-discovery and empowerment, which works best without the rules and self-judgement that your world has taught you. It is a leap of faith, but even a leap of faith can be given a boost through sound perspective. Your journal will develop perspective from your mind, your heart, your soul, and the Goddess working within you. Somewhere along the dreamer's path you must set aside the mask of outward interpretation and simply close your eyes and listen to the quiet of the dreams and the whispers of the Goddess.

You can add the interpretive suggestions provided throughout this book to this foundation of self-knowledge for added dimension, or as possibilities you simply hadn't considered. I hesitate to give concrete dream interpretations simply because dreaming is highly subjective and I am not you. However, symbols can be universal, and it is on that universal substructure—the binding tie of all things—that a relationship with the Goddess and with your dreams is built. This is not an instant process. It requires some time and tenacity, but it's well worth the effort. In the end you'll discover that the worlds of spirit and magick dance through your dream time and you can join in the passionate dance. Create a waking world where dreams come true and the Goddess is alive!

Have patience with yourself, and start dreaming!

One
Daring to Dream

"To sleep, perchance to dream...."

—Shakespeare

I dare you to dream. Like the child on the playground who pushes a friend to run farther, to jump higher—to take what truly exists within and make it manifest—I dare you to dream of the Goddess.

This dare is a pact between you and me: a friendly way of saying, "I know you can do it, and maybe you know you can do it. But, the only way you're going to stretch beyond your own limits is if I point them out as limitations." It's my job to raise the stakes for you; it's your job to prove to yourself that you can do it. Reclaiming the power of dreams is like winning a dare—you're elated, confident, and doing something wonderful for yourself. Beyond the dare, though, is the truth of dreaming. Dreams are the meeting ground between the body, mind, and soul. Together, these Universal pieces make up the dream world with messages of hope, knowledge, understanding, insight, and connection.

"That we come to this earth to live is untrue:
we come but to sleep, to dream."

—Anonymous Aztec poem

Dreams and modern life

It seems as if each day reveals a new self-help book, seminar, or class being held on spirituality, using personal knowledge, or working with dreams for success. Dream journals now sit comfortably on the shelves in major bookstores next to blank books and theme notebooks alike. And yet, with all of these resources, some people find that working with dreams is too much trouble to continue long-term.

The idea that dreams are a waste of time is probably the result of rationalism, a 17th century philosophical movement that emphasized thought and logic over faith and emotions. Let's examine the problem: if dreams hold such valuable knowledge for our lives (as our ancestors believed), why aren't they a priority in modern life? Even the logical mind of today cannot deny a history of over 2,000 years of dream insights and learning.

We manage to place doctor appointments, the gym, family, and business classes in our day timers—why not dreams? Dreams can help answer the universal questions and soothe our fears, but people simply shrug in the morning and forget the dream world. You probably don't even notice it's missing because the next thing on your agenda is looming and you're trying to meet a deadline. Imagine taking a step toward achieving your life's path and having nothing to show for it but sore feet! Dreaming without recognizing the possibility for power and connection with the Goddess in those dreams is getting sore feet for no reason. The habit of letting the world's needs dictate your schedule is easy, but it should be the energy of the Divine and of the Universe that guide you. Dreams can reset your internal compass and keep the rest of the day in focus and on course. It's the larger picture that makes the daily tasks manageable, not the other way around.

Let's examine some of the common reasons modern dreamers have for their absence from the dream world. Maybe you have experienced some of these, maybe not. You can learn a bit, however, about how being "modern" affects your life and how you can make dreaming work for you.

Time is of the essence

By allowing your schedule, and its perceived expectations, to dictate your day, the most important task is forgotten: to understand and listen to the voice of the Divine. It is a common perception that if the body is not actively doing something that you are a slouch and "wasting time." This misconception is at the heart of the modern breakneck pace— and it is not healthy for you. It is not healthy for anyone. Taking time to relax and simply exist as a part of the Universe can't be overestimated. As part of the fabric called the Universe, you have your own unique give-and-take with Universal energy. It's best to let this energy into yourself like a battery, a little at a time (in dreams, meditation, etc.), rather than in one large jolt (seminars, fits of self-improvement) that can shock your system and possibly fry the wiring.

Rather than letting your agenda tell you that you don't have time for dreaming, make certain that you schedule time for reading about dreams, surfing the prolific pages of the Internet, and understanding your own dreams.

"Hunt half a day for a forgotten dream."

—William Wordsworth

Here are a few tips for finding that extra minute for dreams:

- A doctor's waiting room can give you the quiet the dining room table doesn't.

+ An afternoon break at work could be the perfect time to sketch a dream image. (Using the creative half of your mind during regular "logical/ working" time helps you think better about both work and dreams.)

+ Keep your goals realistic: three hours a day spent on dreams isn't practical unless it's your master's thesis. For everyday dreams, 15 minutes will do fine.

+ In the car, talk with family members or friends about your dreams.

+ Occasionally give yourself time off. Schedule a lunch date with yourself and keep it!

+ TV programs are notorious for commercials— an average of eight minutes per half-hour show. In one hour of television you could look over your dream journal, make notes, or finish interpreting a dream.

+ In the morning use a white board marker (the kind that wipe off without window cleaner) and jot down a couple key words from your dreams on the mirror before leaving. Your dream will still be there when you return and have the five minutes to write it down.

Dreams as a waste of time

Science, with its steam engine, industrialization, and medical advances, placed a clock in every home. Time, and the conscious recognition of time's passing, became a constant that guided the household. Life had been improved with revolutionary machines, but the natural rhythm established by the Divine was beginning to take a back seat to time and technology. Dreams fell out of favor because there was already too much to do without "wasting time" on something else.

Working with dreams to find knowledge and enlightenment is an investment back into Nature, the Goddess, and Life. The few minutes you spend in the morning earn interest and energy throughout the day and are returned to you in knowledge and peace. Rather than rushing through your day still disturbed by a dream (consciously or not), spend five minutes writing it in your journal or telling someone you trust. The time you spend will be repaid with a calmer day or some insight into how the stress of your life at the moment could teach important lessons you need to know to follow your path.

"For dreams are always with me...dreams guide me to points I must reach. Dreams are my power, unseen spiritual essence of my soul given substance and made tangible. Through them, healing is possible. Born independently of all my mortal limitations, dreams make me whole, restoring each missing or broken part of me. Then they eloquently speak when my own words are frozen by fear or indecision."

—Ana Lee Walters

The old and the new

Throughout the course of a day the average person will probably use a pager, a cell phone, a computer (laptop or desktop), a telephone, a television, an automobile, and countless other informative and "time-saving" devices. The inventions and advances of the past 100 years have given us rock and roll, walking on the moon, knowledge of world events, global economy, CDs, miraculous medicine, and the Internet. Although efficient, modern life hasn't provided any new tools to help you build a lasting connection to the Goddess. That connection goes beyond both time and technology. Your task is to dust off the dream tools from antiquity (sacred sleep, memory, interpretation, lucid dreams, and insight) and use them alongside the alarm clock, the computer journal, and other technology. We'll do the archaeology for these antique dream tools later, but first consider how these more familiar modern tools can become part of your path toward spiritual dream work with the Goddess. The key is to learn to use these tools from a different perspective (the manufacturer's directions are helpful, but limited in creativity).

- Computer: Possible dream journal; research on dream theories and the Internet.
- Internet: Treasure trove of Web sites to gather information, share dreams, enrich your knowledge of symbols or goddesses, or find expression for art inspired by dreams.
- Cell phone: Waiting on the bus or on lunch are perfect times to call a friend with your dream or leave a summary on your answering machine at home.
- TV: Watch shows that make you think rather than sitcoms and use the wealth of imagery and sound from these shows to build a list of personal symbols.
- Alarm clock: Find one that doesn't use bells, whistles, or buzzers to wake you, but uses steady music or a chime; some clocks have progressive alarms that start softly and get louder. These work great to bring you out of sleep gently.
- Microwave: A note on the microwave to write down dreams will often catch you as you rush out the door with a quick bite to eat.
- Handheld computers: If ever there was a device for dreaming in the modern age, this is it! On the bus or in the plane—you can use it anywhere to record dreams, write reminders of questions you have to resolve in your dream work, sketch an idea, and add calling a friend for dream sharing to your to-do list.

Despite the wonders and "wows" that we get from these modern appliances, remember that caution and moderation are your friends. Each electrical appliance has its own electrical field and too many together can confuse your body's own electromagnetic field. Keeping your brain in tune to the natural order of things means not overloading the circuits of the brain with excess energy.

A short 2,000 years of dreaming

So what does history have to teach you about dreaming? The very first human writings on papyrus and the walls of Egyptian tombs contained dream messages and interpretations, but evidence of sacred dreaming goes even farther back—all the way to 35,000 B.C.E. (Before Common Era) and a sculpture of the Dreamer of Malta. Even one of the great wonders of the world, the Sphinx, is connected to dreams. There is a long history of mankind using dreams for prophecy, wealth, health, and affairs of state and of the heart. While dream practices differed from one group to the next, the belief that dreams were a way of communicating with the Divine is almost universal. Your dreams, with the timeless influence of the Goddess, are as powerful and important as those of the ancients were. As you open your mind to spiritual dreaming, you will begin to touch the beauty known throughout history as the face of the Goddess.

Egypt

Dreams were a part of everyday life for Egyptians, who recorded dreams and their translations with the newly acquired written language. This is the first time that a list of standard meanings was recorded for the interpretation of dreams. For truly sacred dreams, or incubated dreams, people would sleep in the temples of the gods and goddesses. First, the dreamer would be purified and cleansed, and then he would sleep within the temple walls. His dreams were always sacred and special priests at the temple would interpret the dream according to the symbols and ideas sacred to the particular deity of the temple.

Nearly everyone in ancient times relied on the connection and wisdom available in dreams. From the Pharaoh down to the common person, dreams were used to make decisions on everything from planting crops to relationships, wealth, and health. One story relates that Alexander the Great fell ill while in Babylon. He sent his generals to E-Sagila (a temple of Marduk, the Sumerian god of exorcism and healing), where they dreamed a cure for his sickness. The tablet that lies between the feet of the great Sphinx contains the story of Thutmose IV, who encountered an aspect of the god Horus in the dream world. Thutmose's dream revealed that the person who removed the sand that had buried the Sphinx would become a great ruler. Thutmose took this as a suggestion from the Divine and did just that. This kind of instruction from the gods was common in Egyptian dreaming. The placement of temples, sacrifices, fields, houses, and even the planning and execution of wars came under the scrutiny and advice of the gods of Egypt. The dreams of Sumer, Babylon, and Assyria were considered just as important as dreams had been in Egypt, although there was more emphasis on personal deities and individual connection to the Divine.

Rome

Although dreams and dream interpretation enjoyed thousands of years of respectability, a few hundred years of change and a series of key events placed dreaming on the list of disreputable sources of information. At first, the growth of the Holy Roman Empire was a boon to dream goddesses. Along with spices, wealth, and knowledge brought from conquered civilizations, the Romans brought back images of the Divine from the four corners of the globe. Temples and goddesses devoted to dreams thrived throughout the Empire. The Roman gods and goddesses mixed and mingled with their counterparts from Egypt, Persia, and even the Far East.

The temples dedicated to gods and goddesses of dreams were very popular until Emperor Constantine. He dreamed before a battle that if his army were Christian he would win the battle. He and his army converted to Christianity and won the battle. Although his insight came to him in a dream, Emperor Constantine unknowingly began a process that would separate people from their sacred dreams. He declared that the Pagan gods and goddesses, who were not the Christian father-God, were forbidden (including those who specialized in dreams).

Without state sanction, the dream goddesses were shoved out of their place in everyday life. Many people still believed and worshipped the old gods and goddesses, but they did so in secret. Without temples, sacred sleep and priestly interpretation became impossible for the average dreamer. Secrecy, time, and political repression of the Goddess eroded the connection between the people and their belief in the sacred world of dreams. Dreams changed from being the voice of the Divine to being half superstition and half make-believe.

If people didn't believe in dreams and goddesses, what was it that guided them? Rome had replaced their multitude of borrowed gods and goddesses with worship of the Christian God, and now the people replaced inner knowledge with guidance from the priests of the Holy Roman Church. Because the Roman Church controlled most of the universities and writing of the day, it soon became the authority to which most people turned in times of need, much like they had when they looked to dreams and the Goddess.

Christianity and the Holy Roman Empire did much to improve the intellect and science of man, but with the growth of universities and learning came the need to confirm something before you could believe in it. Instead of turning inward to a personal connection to the Goddess, the people turned to the priests, who were the sole connection to divine knowledge. Although sacred dreaming was eventually allowed by the Church as a way that the Lord could reveal himself, it never received the interest and favor that the goddesses and gods of the Pagan world had enjoyed.

Despite centuries of doubt and criticism from established authority figures, people have continued to dream deeply in their personal lives. Civilizations were built on dream insights. Dreamers have continued through public denial, the age of reason, and rationalism to seek the ethereal world between dusk and dawn. History teaches you that you are not alone, that the way may be cluttered and uneasy, but that the rewards can be great.

Dream myths

Although dreams are an innate connection with the Goddess, they connect us to the everyday concerns of life as well. It seems that along with household events, dreams found their place as a rich subject for superstition. Unfortunately, there are just as many superstitions that say a birth is good luck as bad. Most of these superstitions revolve around love, money, happiness, and children—all of which concern modern man. Whether it concerns you personally or not, some of the symbolism (a tornado as a "drain") can be useful when you begin to understand your own dreams and your unique symbols. These ideas, no matter how far-fetched, have been handed down and believed on one level or another for a long time. Thousands of people, over time, have put their personal energy into these superstitions, and using this old-fashioned energy can connect you to these superstitious people.

According to some superstitions, if you dream of:

- Green fields, growing cabbage, or money, you will have good luck or wealth.
- Tornadoes, there will be a death in the family or a person is draining your energy.
- Babies, you will have good luck, no children, a marriage, or a death.
- Things out of season, trouble without reason.
- Death, there will be a birth.
- Being barefoot, you will be carefree or poor.
- Anything and reveal it before breakfast, you will have bad luck.
- Dancing, you will soon have trouble.
- Clear water, there will be happiness.
- Knives, there will be anger and disputes.

Dream Pals

One great false myth is the idea that dreamers always work alone. You may sleep and dream alone, but the rest of your adventure does not have to be solitary. Choose a friend with whom you can share your dreams. Your Dream Pal should be a good listener, have a strong understanding of you, be open to dreaming as a pathway to growth, and be willing to share personal dreams. If your Dream Pal isn't already working on their dreams you might be the nudge they need to begin keeping their own dream journal. A copy of *Dreams of the Goddess* would work well as an invitation to becoming your Dream Pal.

Once you have found your Dream Pal, establish a pattern for your meetings (once a week, every two weeks, and so on). These are your times for sharing, exploring, and interpreting dreams. Perhaps you meet for lunch once a week or over coffee on Thursdays. Whatever the situation, make sure that you are comfortable.

If you find that you are uncomfortable discussing the topics of your dreams, then you may not wish to have a Dream Pal. This is your choice, and on the spiritual path of the dreamer it is your right to maintain your privacy. In this case, your Dream Pal may be the person who simply supports your work with dreams. Perhaps your Pal calls to remind you to take time for dreaming or he sends you a Web site with suggestions for journals. A Dream Pal can help you in a number of ways.

 *Journal*

Recording your dreams in a journal has many benefits. Journals allow you to:

- Revisit your dreams months, years, or decades later for new meanings.
- Review dreams for an outside perspective on the events.
- Prevent the mind, which is not perfect, from inadvertently forgetting important parts or the sequence of events in a dream.
- Compare dreams to each other over the course of time.
- Find recurring themes.

Each section of this book will end with a place for you to continue this conversation on sacred dreaming and to explore your own dreams. Ideas are inert and useless things unless you take them, twist them this way and that, and try them on to find your own perspective on them.

A few notes on journals

Despite the benefits, many dreamers find that keeping a journal gives them flashbacks to high school and the forced journaling of English classes. For these unfortunate journals (a mere shadow of the true possibility for this art form) only legible words were worthwhile, doodling was definitely out, and each day of class you were forced to fill half a page in your journal with something impressive. Talk about pressure! It's not a job or a requirement this time; it's not even an assignment. Outdated concepts of mandatory daily writing, legibility, and lack of creativity might hamper your dream journal if you don't remember one thing: you're in charge now.

The freedom you have earned as an adult should translate into your journal as well; in your dreams and in your dream journal you are the ruler. If you wish to use black paper and fluorescent inks upside down in Greek—great! If you prefer loose-leaf notebook paper and a clipboard, then find an office supply store. If you choose to record all of your dreams or just a selection, this is also your decision. Your journal will become a reminder and a connection point between you and your sacred dream space. The pages within your journal will also become sacred space in a sense. If you are uncomfortable with the physical nature of a journal (spiral bound journals are often uncomfortable for left-handed dreamers), you will be less likely to use your journal and therefore, it will be less likely you will connect with the Goddess you seek.

Your journal can take any form you want, including three-dimensional. You are only limited by your own power to decide what you want in a journal. One woman used magazine clippings and images from junk mail in order to create collages in her journal (a fabulous way to reuse this refuse). A glue stick, a pair of scissors, and a few moments was all it took for her journal to become a very visual representation of her hopes, fears, and dreams. She also filled in a few words of description about details in her dreams, but the majority of her record was visual. Consider adding ribbons, pictures, small pieces of cloth, e-mail, items from the Internet, or other things that might represent the emotions and ideas within your dreams. You might also include notes on dreaming in general, resources for later, or symbolism.

One strong suggestion for reading the journal section in each chapter: take it slowly. Personal exploration and developing a relationship with the Goddess both need to be done with respect for the natural order of things. A firm foundation is the goal, not mass production. Each chapter's journal section has three or four journal prompts (each one is titled and followed by a brief description or instruction) that are your food for thought. I suggest reading a journal prompt and then leaving the idea in the back of your mind, like a ball of dough. In the right conditions (warm, accepting, open mind), the ball of ideas will rise and double in size. Often the best "thinking" is done when your conscious mind is busy doing other tasks such as driving, crafts, or cooking. The repetition of daily routine is an easy form of meditation. Take advantage of the opportunities you have for this kind of meditation. If you are the person who cooks dinner, keep your journal on a corner of the countertop. Then, when an idea strikes, you can jot down a couple of key words or sketch an idea from your dream the night before.

The rules of Journals

Rule #1: There are no rules to journaling—anything goes.

Rule #2: Write in your journal only as often as you want. Forget the idea that it needs to be every day.

Rule #3: You must write in a form that records your dreams and effectively communicates the ideas within the dream. Grammatically correct sentences aren't necessary. (Although legible writing does help after time has faded the dream's memory for you.) If lists of key words or sketches of people work better for you, then use those.

Rule #4: Use your own words to describe your dream. Many times in journal entries you might be tempted to phrase things in the politically correct terms that society uses. Ideas and feelings occur to you in strong, personal terms. Use these rather than the toned down words that have passed through "society's filters." There are no filters necessary in your dream journal.

Rule #5: Claim the space in your journal as private. Let the people around you know that you are learning about yourself and your dreams. Make sure they know that it is important that you do this in the private spaces of your journal. Letting your friends and family know ahead of time about your journal can avoid their fear of the unknown. Journals are as sacred as the thoughts in your mind. Your mind is part of what makes you human. To take away this freedom of thought (or to invade someone's mind through their journal) is to deny a person the freedom to be human and an individual.

If someone does accidentally open the front cover, make sure they know what they are doing. I encourage you to write a strong personal statement on the outside cover of your journal. For example: "This is the personal dream journal of Sarah. I write this journal as an extension of myself. Please show this piece of me the respect you have for all of me." The statement should let the casual observer know that this is your private space.

Rule #6: Record only information that is important to you. Faithfully recording a dream by your standards will keep your journal meaningful to you. You should, however, record some information about when you had your dream. The following is a list of suggested items that you can include for the header of a dream. You may use some, all, or none of these in your own journal:

- Calendar date (month, day, year).
- Time of dream.
- Title of dream (a short idea that will remind you of the dream's content).
- Place you were sleeping (city, state, friend's house, etc.).
- Phase and astrological sign of the moon. (The moon moves through all of the signs every cycle. Each astrological sign affects dreams differently.)

- Major events from the preceding day and the day ahead.
- Weather conditions (especially rain and the temperature).
- Your physical condition (healthy, sore throat, and so on).
- People nearby (in your home).

Modern musings

Wherever you are reading this book, stop and look around you. You are somewhere that is probably familiar—an office, your home, or maybe in a parked car. What evidence of technology do you see around you? (Include things such as streetlights, cars, computers, watches, etc.) Humans have progressed in many ways, some good and some bad. In this journal entry, make a list of five or six of these items and consider how these modern conveniences affect your daily life. Which of these items provides the greatest benefit for you? Why? Do any of these items increase your connection with others? What about your connection to the Divine? Do they limit your connections?

Lifestyle check

Equipment isn't the only obstacle as you begin your search for the Goddess within your dreams. Your lifestyle gives your life an outline and form. Some people have noted that they rush through the daily concerns of life without enjoying the important parts—family, friends, and spiritual fulfillment. Using half of this journal space, describe "A day in the life of me." Include your to-do list for the day, your "hats" of responsibility (parent, employee, spouse, sibling, child, housekeeper, cook, handyman, etc.), and your feelings throughout the day. When you began the day, were you hopeful? Were you satisfied at the end of the day or maybe apprehensive during a meeting? Once you have recorded a typical day, spend one day during your week trying to be consciously aware of your time, activities, and feelings. Use the other half of your journal space to record this "conscious day." Remember: You are your own natural resource. Did you renew yourself with personal time during the day? What portion of your day was spent on mundane, daily activities (laundry, work, etc.) and what portion was spent on self-development or spirituality? Does your lifestyle currently hold a place for the Goddess?

Dreams

Record in detail any dreams you have over a period of a week. If you don't remember your dreams, write down the events or situations that might have prevented you from remembering the dreams. Remember to include feelings, thoughts, places, actions, and whatever else you can think of.

The balance sheet

List the obstacles (physical, mental, or situational) that limit your ability to remember and work with your dreams. Choose one or two of the most difficult obstacles and explore exactly how that item prevents you from remembering and cherishing your dreams.

For example: *TV—doesn't encourage individual thought, gives input but does not allow output of information, "couch potato syndrome," and escapist entertainment.* Suggest one or two solutions to each of these problems. For example: *One evening a week (or just a couple hours) without TV can increase the things I accomplish immensely.*

Carefully review your journal entries so far and your life overall for items, people, places, and opportunities that can help you embrace your dreams for personal growth. Perhaps you can use the 10 minutes before everyone arrives home to focus your mind on a dream or a symbol from the day. Be creative. List these assets clearly. You might begin by stating that, *(Item) can support my divine dreaming by allowing me to___.*

Two
The Goddess Within

There are many movements in the modern metaphysical world to look back at history and learn from the past. History, as the saying goes, is a great teacher. Thousands of years can teach you unfathomable things, but today you should focus only on dreams and their connection with the Goddess. Your dreams are connected through millions of starry nights to the dreams of people on every continent and the Goddesses that have blessed and protected those peoples. Japan, Persia, Egypt, Germany, Ireland, Chile, Brazil, South Africa, and the United States all trace dreaming farther back than memory and written records. Before there were texts and scholars to record dreams and interpretations, there were friends and families to pass on the myths and superstitions surrounding dreams.

A short history of the Goddess

This is a history of the Goddess, her images and her dreams rather than the more traditional history of places and events.

The Venus collection

Before the invention of the wheel, before the continents had finished shifting over the Earth's surface, the Goddess was recognized by Her people as the greatest of beings. The face of the Goddess may have changed over time, but Her presence and importance to the balance of life continues, unbroken. The first images of the Goddess did not even have a face. The Venus of Willendorf (as She is called today) was a straightforward appeal by the earliest humans to the raw power of the Goddess. She was seen as the life force of everything—animals, plants, and humans. These people were part of the Cycle of Life that carried them forward from birth to life to death and back again to rebirth. The Goddess controlled these great forces.

Imagine you are looking at the world in 42,000 B.C.E., when people have just learned to use tools. This world of life and death is personified by the Goddess figure, whose burgeoning belly contains not only a child, but the future of the clan. Her abundant breasts symbolize Her strength in feeding Her children—you. The circle of seven braids (a sacred number) obscures Her face and reminds you that She is not a woman, but *every* woman.

The birth, life, and death of the animals and seasons are the movement of the Divine in the Paleolithic world. In this world, you would recognize that you are not outside of the seasons and the Cycle of Life, but you are a part of that Cycle. You are part of the Divine's body as Nature. From the depths of your heart you would seek to honor the place the Divine holds for you and the tribe by carving and carrying an image of the Great Goddess. Made of clay, the Venus of Willendorf is a reminder that the human form may be Divine, but it is also fragile.

There are no user's manuals and online customer support to tell you what the Willendorf Goddess meant, exactly, to the

Paleolithic man who fashioned Her. But some things seem fairly clear. Even before recorded history the individual felt the personal presence of the Goddess. Because great care was taken not to damage the fragile figure, she was probably of great value. Whatever conclusions you draw from her simple form, it seems that a desire to connect to the patterns of Life and the Divine moved early man.

The Venus of Willendorf is the oldest image carved by man found to date, but she is by no means alone as the face of the Goddess in prehistoric times. Other carvings of women, also called "Venuses," were discovered from the late Paleolithic era in places as diverse as France, Spain, Russia, and Siberia. One of the most interesting carvings is the Venus of Laussel (dated 25,000 to 20,000 B.C.E.), a limestone carving above a doorway. She is holding a horn or crescent moon with 13 slashes, which represent the 13 lunar cycles, and her other hand points to her belly. Both the crescent in the figure's hand and the 13 slashes connect this goddess closely with the moon. The Goddess (through the moon's effects on the fertility cycle of women) has carried responsibility for the procreation of mankind since the very beginning of time. The connection of the Goddess to the moon and to the lunar cycle continues into today to remind you that Her power is real, it is now, and it is available for you. It is not a coincidence that the moon is the guardian of the night and the symbol of many goddesses. Night is the dreamer's world and the realm of the Goddess. The fertility and creativity of mankind's ancestors is still available to you during your dreams. Your dreams are guided and protected each night by the Goddess in the form of the gentle warmth of the moon.

> *"There is a dream dreaming us."*
>
> —A Kalahari Bushman

The Dreamer of Malta

One of the first records of sacred dreaming is recorded in a delicate sculpture from the late Paleolithic period, known as the *Dreamer of Malta*. The shamanic woman in this carving reclines on a formal bed in order to receive divine dreams from the Goddess. The sculpture is dated approximately 3,000 B.C.E. and is the first recorded evidence of a belief in dreams and their power to connect with the Divine.

Again, the Dreamer of Malta leaves very few written accounts of her purpose and function, but she does reveal another face of the Goddess as seen so long ago—the face that is peaceful in sleep. Found in a temple devoted to dreaming, the figure suggests that one form of worship common to the ancient people of Malta was that of sacred sleep. Sacred sleep is the intentional use of night, dreaming, and sleep as a form of connection and communion with the power of the Divine. As early man looked to the trees and the seasons or to the Venus of Willendorf, these peoples looked within their dreams to touch the face of the Goddess.

For the Dreamer of Malta, the Goddess resided deep within the visions of the night, a world of dreams that runs like a still, deep river along the history of mankind and forward into its future. The dreamworld that connected the island people of

Malta to their Goddess also connects to you. The Goddess carries with Her the knowledge of these people. She carries insight, perspective, hope, possibility, health, foresight, and all things unimagined. Special tools are not required to reach this knowledge, only the peaceful restorative dreaming that was given by the Goddess as part of the nature of being human. You are beginning the reclaiming of that power now, through the reclaiming of the Goddess.

The Goddess gets a Neolithic make-over

Time passed; the Paleolithic era came to an end; and the nature of life changed for man. Two distinct lifestyles emerged as the Neolithic era began, and the form of the Goddess kept up with the times. The face of the Venus changed and grew with the needs of Her people. Divine images throughout history have served as a reflection of the changing concerns of people. For Neolithic people, their belief and connection to the force that moved within their lives was constant, but the two halves of humanity (the farmers and the nomads) related differently to the Divine. The two halves of humanity had gained separate perspectives on the world and the Goddess.

The farmers needed a Goddess of abundance, patience, and constant cycles that brought the nutrients for their crops. During the time of the first farmers, the Goddess took the form of a Divine power over the rivers and the lives of the valley dwellers. She also gained responsibility for the crops and the newly domesticated farm animals. People saw in the pull and flow of the river (the most powerful force in their lives) the same cycle that governs a woman's body. Thus, the Divine force of the rivers became known as the Goddess of the River. Each place had its own Goddess: Djao Phraya (Maenam River in Thailand), Anuket (Nile River in Egypt), Boann (Boyne River in Ireland), Oxshun (Nigerian river Goddess), Ganga (Ganges River in India), and the Mesopotamian snake

Goddess. Even today there are rivers around the world that retain the name of their patron goddesses.

The nomads continued to hunt and gather for their food as their ancestors had, and they struggled for survival against the elements. For these cave-dwelling people, the power of the hunt was more important than the fertility of the land. For these hunters, the Divine image remained animistic and mostly male, but there were a few fertility goddesses for these strong nomads to rely on. The face of the Goddess as the face of Nature did not change much from earlier times for the Nomads. It was the basic elements of fire, weather, and warfare that were depicted on cave walls as flame, swords, or lightning bolts. These were some of the first images of strictly male dieties; a reflection of the need for strength and power by the nomadic peoples.

Two worlds collide

Around 5,000 B.C.E. the first evidence of warfare began to scar the face of the Goddess's world. Warfare became an art for the nomads because taking from others was sometimes easier than finding food and supplies in a land that was not always kind.  The farmers had learned to store their crops and the nomads, had learned that agriculture made the farmers people almost defenseless. Generations of domesticated animals and stationary crops had separated the farmers from their skills as hunters and warriors. Nomads, desperate for supplies and food, raided the farming societies in the rich river valleys.

After conquering a village, nomadic warriors would stay to maintain control over the people. They would marry, have children, and begin lives as new residents of the town. In a similar fashion, the gods and goddesses of the two societies married. As a village was conquered, the myths and stories that surrounded the local goddess would change to reflect the life of her followers. A goddess could be captured, fall in love, or be married to a distant prince, but generally the stories reflected the union of the two peoples and the permanent nature of the change. Rarely did the God figure from the nomadic warriors completely supplant the Goddess, but often the God would defeat any paramour or consort.

The Goddess remained an intricate part of this early world despite fundamental changes in both technology and life. Her power and personal connection enabled the Goddess to transcend the events of the day and speak to the people about the events of the Universe. She carries the same messages for you today.

> *We all come from the Goddess*
> *And to Her we shall return*
> *Like a drop of rain*
> *Flowing to the ocean.*
>
> —Modern chant that speaks about the importance of the Goddess

The family of the Goddess grows

The marriage of the nomadic God and the agricultural Goddess in these cultures eventually brought about a family of deities. The Goddess and Her mate became part of the cosmic cycle when their union produced children. As older Gods had younger Gods, the roles and powers of each deity changed. The older Goddesses ruled as powerful river Goddesses and Earth Mother figures. The children Gods and Goddesses ruled over specific aspects of life that concerned the new city dwellers.

Imagine that you are standing in the doorway of a small home in Jericho or Troy between the Bronze and Iron Ages. The economy is still strongly based on agriculture, oil lamps are a new item in Sumeria, and chicken is a recently domesticated animal used for food. Looking out across the city, you are concerned that the new sickness will affect your children, that if a band of raiders came the food supply would not last, or that the people in power might make a decision that would put your bakery out of favor. These new needs are expressed to the Goddess, and she answers in the form of the children Gods. Some of these lesser Goddesses ruled over healing, communication, love, dreams, and the arts and sciences. Even though the face of the Goddess changed, grew, and divided into many new forms, Her connection with and protection of Her people continued.

Her face became the familiar ones of Roman, Greek, Egyptian, and Sumerian Goddesses, as well as those from other regions. She was dressed in the clothes of her people. With the advent of weaving the Goddess donned the loose robes of the wealthy and carried the overflowing cornucopia of the irrigated fields. Wisdom, grace, insight, courage, love, and wealth were the bounties of her people. Because the life of the people included city-states and male dominant rulers, the world of the Divine began to include an overseeing husband-father God.

> *"Dreaming is an act of pure imagination, attesting in all men a creative power, which, if it were available in waking, would make every man a Dante or Shakespeare."*
>
> —H. F. Hedge

The dark hour of the Goddess

Civilization brought about many changes within human culture, and the Goddess walked along each step of the way. But as reason replaced a personal connection to the Divine, and goddesses were placed in history books, the world slowed its growth to a crawl and began a period known as The Dark Ages. It was during these dark ages that the face of the Goddess found its saddest expression.

The unashamed strength, power, and fertility of the Paleolithic Venus Goddesses are hard to trace in the lines of the more modern "companion" Goddesses, but they are there. Shifting Her position from one of independence to one of association, the Goddess became distant from Her people. The temples of Crete that held vast statues and altars were destroyed as bands of raiders carried away what was of value: the gold carvings, statues, and offerings. The true robbery, however, was not the looting of the temples. The greatest loss was the newly absent relationship between the Energy of Creation and the individual. Instead of a positive, powerful relationship that influenced both the supplicant and the Goddess, the newly formed invader/invaded communities began to fear a God of control and war. A relationship based on fear and consequences is not one that encourages an open heart, and it is only through openness that the voice of the Goddess can be heard. Her voice whispered only in dreams and hidden hearts during these dark times.

The God of the invaders is, however, not to be dismissed out of hand. He provided strength during a time when mankind was uncomfortably shifting from an individual connection to the Divine to the centralized religion where a trained priest acted as intermediary. When Jehovah forced the Goddess to speak in a quiet voice, he provided structure and promises of protection to replace Her. It was the introduction of the Christian God to Rome that marked the strongest shift in the Goddess's image to date.

Rome, with its armies and inventions for warfare, was the most successful conquering "tribe"; but in the end, the great Roman Empire could only minimize the Goddess—she was not to be conquered. Outposts and Roman roads were found as far apart as Ireland and India, along with Goddesses from nearly every region of the globe. Each new territory brought with it a new system of beliefs, a new "outfit" for the Goddess; gold, and white for the Egyptian Isis or the earthy color of rushes for the Irish Brigid. Regardless of the clothing, the image was the same.

The Goddess who was once face-less to reflect Her difference from us was given features and a likeness that was so similar to that of people that our connection to Her was undeni-able. The image of the Goddess be-came something familiar, friendly, and easier to visualize as a piece of  Divinity that could be concerned with the everyday. So, dressed in the Roman toga, the Goddess stood to the side and slightly below the gods whose altars cluttered Rome.

The marketplace of the world's goddesses that was ancient Rome was destined for a long and busy partnership with the Roman military, but something changed. Emperor Constantine converted to Christianity and all other Gods were banned from Rome. Christianity did not kill the Goddess during this tur-bulent time, and she can be seen clearly in the face of the Virgin Mary. More quiet and subdued than some of the God-desses before her, the Virgin still speaks to the world of peace, fertility and hope. She is the symbol by which man acknowl-edges the un-Earthly power of divine creation.

The timeless Goddess

History is a wonderful teacher, but the Goddess isn't stuck in a long-ago past that has no resemblance to your living room. Like a mother's heart in the womb, the pulse of the Goddess is a sound that is familiar and comforting, a sound that carries across time without changing. The Goddess, and your con-nection to Her, are the powerful tools that will help to sustain and guide you in the present, just as she supported your an-cestors in the past. Her existence hasn't changed, only her names. Whether your ancestry is European, African, Celtic, or of the Orient, the Goddess has danced with you in the past and into the present.

The Goddess is not any one person. She is not the Willendorf Goddess, Isis, or the Virgin Mary. She is greater than these names. She is the life force of the Universe, the womb of your life. She is the Creatrix and the Source. In life itself we always have a reminder because everyone has a mother, everyone is connected to the cycle of Nature that perpetuates life. In living, you participate in this cycle and move your own life forward, becoming your own mother, your own Goddess.

The male aspect of Life, called God by innumerable traditions, provides the spark that is the energy and motion of Life. The substance and sustenance of life are from the Goddess. Together they form a balance that is the constant Cycle of Life. Even in cultures where the Goddess was most prevalent, she had consorts and partners that balanced Her energy. With the body of the world and no spark, the source that begins and keeps things in motion cannot function properly. Likewise, the spark of the God without the nurturing of the Goddess is an incomplete system. It is the nurturing of your relationship with the Goddess that can heal and guide you, even in the modern world that seems tipped toward the God's powers.

The Goddess embodies the moon waxing full, the ebb and flow of the tides, and human curiosity. She is possibility and nurturing love. In the face of the ever-reasoning, step-by-step energy of the male God, it is often hard for modern dreamers to make leaps of pure faith, powerful creativity, and enlightened spirituality. Thus, it is necessary to bring the Goddess into the equation to help balance the scales. Within the dreamworld the Goddess can help you discover your inner self and answer your questions. She can restore your balance with the brilliant force of Life.

This connection doesn't have to be intense and awesome every time. If every moment were an ecstasy of enlightenment we wouldn't finish getting up in the morning! Our part of the Universe is to continue living, to move forward with life in whatever form is yours. It's not easy to go to meetings and pick up home improvement supplies if you're taking in the wonders of the Universe. But for the seeker and dreamer, if awe isn't the goal, then what purpose is there for maintaining a connection to the Goddess? What kind of connection can you have and still live effectively?

Simply noting the influence of the Goddess on life is enough to maintain a connection to Her and achieve a balance, and it won't stop you from enjoying Life. Whether you note the beauty of a loved one's face or the Cycle of Life as an animal dies to feed another animal, just being open to these observations is a beginning. The awareness of things around you can deepen your enjoyment of Life as well as intensify the Life within you.

So remember to smile a "thank you" when the flowers remind you of the Goddess's blessings, but remember to keep doing your part in Her world. Honoring Her gift of dreams is another easy "thank you."

Your dreams are one of the strongest daily connections you can have to the Goddess. Sweet dreams!

Journal

Symbols of men and women

The most prominent element of dreams is the imagery, and what those images represent can tell us about our thoughts; this is a process called symbolism. Think about the images associated with men and women in the modern world. The easy ones include the symbol for male and female (circles, one with an arrow for male and with a plus sign for female), the variety of figures on bathroom doors, or even specific clothing (skirts, suits, etc.). (This exercise works well with clippings from newspapers and magazines.) In a separate notebook, sketch or describe as many of these symbols as you can. For each symbol, leave enough space to list two things: the traditional meaning assigned to the picture by society and your own personal interpretation. These two perspectives can be the same, similar, or completely different. It is important to recognize the symbols that surround you and their influence on your thinking. For example, a pair of gloves on a woman can suggest delicate feminine traits to one person, while suggesting severe judgement to another person, as in the "white glove" test. On a man, gloves are generally only part of a uniform (a symbol of power).

Dream Pals

Over the course of a week have your Dream Pal note male/
female images and symbols around him. In your meeting this
week compare these images and figures. Note that each person
will probably have slightly different symbols and forms as they
move from the concrete (bathroom door symbols) to the ab-
stract. This difference is the power of the individual to interpret signs. This is a power you wield in the dream world.

Images of the Goddess

Try looking at the descriptions of the ancient goddesses in this book, from other sources, or in your own home. For one or two goddesses, sketch a rough idea of her image next to a short list of the attributes you feel she has (even if it's just ideas associated with her—the goddess Caffeina would have a coffee cup). This is a list that begins with the idea "when I look at her, I think about...." Remember that the goddesses aren't going to get their feelings hurt. If you feel a figure is unattractive or weird, acknowledge that. The Great Mother goddesses are sometimes symbolized by fruit, bowls, chalices, wine, grain, milk, and the moon. The Earth goddesses from early times often resemble mountains or features of the Earth.

Once you have looked at two or three goddesses, take a moment and look again at your sketches. Does the first goddess look like a chalice or clock? Does she remind you of another object? Another person? Look around your home and office for inspiration in this department. By looking at the forms and symbols associated with women and with goddesses, you should begin to be more aware of these symbols in your waking life. Note how many of these symbols you see where you are sitting now, while you are at work, or during the course of the day. How many of those images have positive associations for you? Neutral? Negative?

Dreams of the Goddess

As you record your dreams over the next week or two, note any dreams that have Goddess images or an overall theme related to Her. Because each goddess has different aspects of the Divine, one dream may contain a fertile field that opens to accept the crops and hopes of a civilization, while another dream may reflect the protectiveness of a Celtic goddess. If you are unsure about whether a dream has Goddess images, trust your instincts. You may not be able to pinpoint the symbol or reference, but perhaps at a later time you will. Write down the dream and a note about your instinctual feelings; this will remind you of the connection to the Goddess and Her influence may become clear.

Opening a place

Before you begin the work of reconnecting with the Goddess, a little bit of symbolic housecleaning might be in order. Imagine that you are at lunch with your friends and you are discussing your recent journey toward sacred dreaming. How do you explain your new adventure? Are you strong and confident in expressing your personal growth, or are your words understated? What fears, inhibitions, or negative thoughts would prevent you from openly discussing your dreams of the Goddess? Write down these "dust bunnies" and make a note of the source as internal (doubts from within your own heart) or external (friends or ideas outside of you who have created negative situations).

_____

_____

_____

_____

Once your concerns and obstacles have been listed, concentrate on the internal issues because these are the only ones you have complete control over. In situations where the source of the problem is outside of you, then your control is limited. Look at each item separately and try to find the source of your discomfort. A fear of ridicule might result from previous experiences with a friend, and one solution might be to discuss your dreams with a more accepting friend.

Symbolically cleaning up these doubts will help the process of opening to the Goddess. Make two columns on a separate piece of paper. In one column, list the obstacles to your dreams and spiritual connection to the Goddess, and in the second column list your affirmation that will address the issue (stated positively). The words "no," "not," "never," and "but" should *not* appear in your affirmation.

For example: (column 1) *I am afraid of being laughed at, or being told to "get serious."* (column 2) *The happiness of myself and my Spirit are important matters deserving respect. I will treasure the act of dreaming as a way of respecting myself.*

Tear the paper into strips for each obstacle (to handle things one at a time) and then again between the obstacle and the affirmation (to cut away the parts you do not want to keep). Keep the affirmations on your bedside (or under your pillow in an envelope) for one complete cycle of the moon. Read these affirmations at least once a week. Old habits will not change overnight and most dreamers need the gentle reminder. Your obstacles should be symbolically returned to the Earth by burying them (where appropriate), burning them in a fireplace, or writing them in sand left out in the wind.

Letter to the Goddess

Write a letter to the Goddess that follows the traditional prayer pattern of addressing the Divine: asking for help and then thanking for help and guidance. As you address the Goddess, describe the aspects that attract you or connect you to Her. Include Her name and description, if you know it. Once you have Her attention, gently ask for the answer to your needs. If you are unsure of what will fill your needs (specifically those related to dreaming) or would like to leave the type of help up to the Goddess, then simply describe your needs and desires for dreaming. Once you have accomplished this, remember to acknowledge the power you place in the hands of the Goddess for helping you in Life. Thank Her for any attention or assistance that She might offer and acknowledge your connection to Her. By honoring the pieces of the Goddess you see within yourself and in the outside world, you draw yourself closer to Her power and the Cycle of Life.

Three

Rosemary for Remembrance

The key to unlocking the dream world and strengthening your connection to the Goddess begins with remembering your dreams. This sounds simple in theory. If you can't remember your dreams, then interpreting the message from the Gods will be like trying to read a letter that has been written in invisible ink—useless! Some dreamers choose to ignore their dreams, while other dreamers treasure the nightly escapades of the mind. If you're reading this book, you're probably in the second category and well on your way to success.

Despite your desire to honor the place of the dream among your personal tools, you will face the same challenges and obstacles as everyone else—reality. Whether those obstacles are physical, mental, spiritual, or situational, there are ways of stepping around and past each one. Take your guidance from the Hindu God Ganesha, the "remover of obstacles." As an elephant-headed man, he crushes some of the obstacles while his companion mouse goes under, through, and around them. However you approach each obstacle, the first step is recognizing the source of problems you might have remembering your dreams.

"Dreaming is the inner language of the soul through which wisdom is transmitted to our conscious minds."

—Arthur Bernard

Obstructions in your dream path

With every journey there are similar steps: you choose a destination; map your way along known and unknown roads; and then put one foot in front of the other until you reach the goal. Remembering your dreams is very similar. If you are trying to remember your dreams, then your goal is clear and easily defined. But what about mapping out the road ahead? What stands between you and remembering your dreams? There are many paths to each destination, and the path to remembering your dreams is no different. These are some suggestions that I have used in my dream work, but if you are inspired to try something else—go for it! As your relationship with dream work and the Goddess develops you will create your own patterns and style of dreaming. Even in dreaming we retain our individuality.

The body knows

During waking hours, your body performs many functions (talking, walking, and even driving) that rely on the body's memory of past actions. Your muscle memory allows you to perform these actions without thinking, and you know instantly if something is amiss because it "feels" out of place. The same kind of physical memory can give you clues to your dreams. Your obstacle is the habit of immediately stretching, rushing for the bathroom, or checking the time. Each of these activities changes the posture, tension, and composition of your body as it rests in the bed and reduces your chance of remembering your dream.

The most universal example of physical memory is the person who has been under stress and realizes that the muscles around their neck and shoulders are tight (or even clenching your jaw as you sleep). The tension that others want to avoid in their bodies can be a physical reminder of your dreams and emotions. Waking with tense muscles might signal stress that is worrying you subconsciously. Waking with your legs stretched out in all directions might let you know that your dream was a good one.

One technique that has worked for other dreamers is a quick and easy check you can use at waking. By the time you have debated on whether you can hit the snooze button, you could have taken a huge leap forward toward remembering your dreams "by head, heart, and hands." This simple method will enable you to make use of the valuable time between sleeping and fully waking. Keep in mind that because it is a physical technique done as you wake up, it might take several days of practice. Just keep practicing and know that it will become habit, just as many other things in your physical life do.

By head, heart, and hands

As you awake, lie still for the count of three slow breaths. During those breaths you should do a short mental self-check of your body to find out what your body remembers from the dream world. Remember to note your impressions in your journal once you are up and moving.

- ◆ *Head* (your mental state): Does your mind seem to be clear and logical, or confused and overwhelmed? If you remember a dream, make a mental note of a key idea, object, or scene that summarizes the basic ideas of the dream.
- ◆ *Heart* (your emotional/spiritual state): Are you scared, neutral, excited, invigorated, apathetic, angry, etc.? Is your heart rate normal, slow, or racing? Do you feel one emotion or several at one time? If there are several emotions, note as many of the strong ones as possible.

- *Hands* (your body's state): Note where your hands are in relation to each other: Are they separated, palms together, clenched, or relaxed? What about the position of the rest of your body? Include how your body feels and whether this is a natural sleeping position.

In the next three breaths, reinforce the ideas you have just reviewed. All together, this exercise will take about a minute to complete—a brief but crucial time in remembering dreams. Take this brief minute to do a check-up, and know that you have saved yourself 15-20 minutes of worry and struggle later in the day trying to remember what you felt and thought just at the moment of waking.

> *"I've dreamt in my life of dreams that have stayed with me ever after, and changed my ideas: they've gone through and through me, like wine through water, and altered the color of my mind."*
>
> —Emily Brontë

A mind prepared for dreams

The same objections surface from dreamers in every area of life. The most common complaints are:
- I have more "important" responsibilities.
- No one else believes me.
- It's too much trouble.
- I'm too rushed in the mornings.
- I always forget.

If any of these excuses seem familiar, then you share some obstacles with other dreamers. When you approach the idea of dreaming (or engaging in any activity that is centered on your personal and spiritual growth), it is easy to find excuses to stop searching. Each excuse is an opportunity to examine your world and discover obstacles that keep dreaming and the

Goddess at bay. Listen to the inner voices that object to dreaming and make note of the things they say because these will be your biggest obstacles.

Simply saying that you want to open the power of dreams in your life is not enough. Each day a little effort is required to reinforce the pattern of waking slowly, remembering, and then recording a dream. Outward attitudes aren't always the same as the ideas that are carried about in our hearts, and a dreamer-to-be who says he's tried everything may not have tried calming the doubt in his own mind. The most common problems—doubt and insecurity—actually come from inside the dreamer.

Don't let the assumption that dreaming is time-consuming (or any of the other false assumptions) keep you from using this tool to grow and explore with the Goddess. Aside from the idea that dreaming takes lots of time, would-be dreamers frequently assume that journals have to be kept daily, that everything needs interpretation, or that dreams are simply something that happens to us rather than something in which we participate. Unfortunately, these are conclusions that can be reached if you do not examine the real source of your obstacles. Take your time at the end of this chapter with the journal exercises that focus on assumptions and obstacles. By seeking the dream world you have acknowledged that spiritual growth is important to you. Use the power of this need to remove your obstacles.

Reserve your spirit's energy

In a world that pushes forward, upward, and onward at every turn, you can feel pressured to be and do everything. Each task and responsibility demands a portion of your daily energy, both physical and spiritual. While physical energy will suffice for most tasks (going to work, meetings, cleaning house), other tasks require insight and perspective that is only available to you with a strong source of spiritual energy. Physical energy is easy to fix with food and rest, but spiritual energy requires a lot more to replenish.

Imagine that you are a water cistern. For each task before you, whether it is washing dishes or balancing a checkbook, you are drained a little. It is essential to your spiritual growth that the level within the cistern be maintained. Without a source of water, your energy cistern will become empty and be of service to no one. Recognizing that your spiritual energy is incredibly important, and that dreams provide a source to refresh that energy, can put dreams on the daily to-do list without causing an additional burden. Dreams are the way you can get the energy to do the rest of the things on your list.

Our minds are tricky beings, however, and old habits die slowly. To move your mind from its old patterns to new ones (and to circumvent the excuses that become obstacles to dreaming), try the following spell.

Spell for replenishing the waters of life

Fill your favorite glass (one that allows you to see the water) with filtered water to the halfway level. Set the glass in a place where it will be undisturbed but where you can still see it frequently. The glass represents you—beautiful, whole, and open to possibilities. The water is the energy you hold within you each day.

- Each morning during the week take a moment with your glass and say the following prayer. When you are giving energy, pour some of the water out or onto a plant. When you are renewed with energy, refill the glass.

- "Goddess, I contain energy that I can change with my mind (swirl the glass). I calm my energy with centering (hold glass still). Today, I will devote my energy to (list your responsibilities and tasks for the day—work, family, a personal project). I will also remember to give energy to remembering my dreams. These dreams will renew me and link me to you."

• As you progress through the week, the water should continue to fill your glass after each prayer. Be aware of the level in the glass and your own energy. By the end of the week, the glass should be completely full. Some water will evaporate, but that shouldn't worry you. You use energy that you don't recognize each day and the evaporated water reminds you of that.

• At the end of the week, take the water to a plant or into your yard and pour it out saying, "This water is part of me, and part of the cycle of energy that moves through the world. I return this energy to the cycle so that it may return to me. May the Goddess grant that my glass always be full."

This exercise will help you remember that energy is something you can manipulate, that it can be used to fill your roles and responsibilities, and most importantly that you need to find a way to renew that energy for yourself. The Goddess can become your well of energy. Lacking enough energy is just one obstacle to dreaming. Your path as a successful dreamer is the one that looks only at one obstacle at a time, like taking just one step instead of an entire journey at once. Finding the courage to step around each obstacle is a sign of your growing strength; remember to celebrate this progress.

Sacred dream space

The temple of the body

Before you can begin to create sacred space, you must first create comfortable space for dreaming. All sleep is not created equal, and it is actually REM sleep (during the last portion of your dream cycle) that promotes the kind of dreaming you need to feel rejuvenated. If you are not reaching REM sleep regularly, then you are most likely not benefiting from your dreams.

Sleeping deeply is not an automatic thing, and the comfort of our bodies while we sleep affects our dreams and our ability to remember those dreams. If your movements are confined by the weight of family pets or constricting covers, then the dream world will reflect that with dreams of chains, weights, and conflict. In order to connect with your sacred dreams and the Goddess, the nagging of your body should be minimized, if possible. Fortunately, you have some control over this obstacle. Here is a list of things that might be restricting your comfort:

- Mattress and pillow: You need to have support without lying on rocks. Consider adding a supportive layer of foam, a better pillow, a new set of sheets, or even turning the mattress over.

- Temperature: Your sleeping room should be two or three degrees cooler than you prefer for lounging around the house. Breathing cool air encourages the body to breathe deeply and will increase the oxygen you have available during sleep.

- Companions: Animals and family members who sleep with you for comfort can create a sense of closeness—but maybe too close. Find a compromise sleeping arrangement for times when you wish to intentionally seek your sacred dreams.

- Clothing: Reconsider your favorite flannel pajamas. Try to keep your nightwear light, loose, and comfortable.

- Physical discomfort: If you suffer from stress, chronic back pain, or other physical discomforts, then sleeping deeply is probably not an easy task. Take time to do what helps: relax your neck muscles; stretch slowly; take a warm shower; put a pillow between your knees to ease back pain; or maybe even get a chiropractic adjustment. The object is to limit the attention your body demands from you while sleeping.

Temple teachers

Large estates, temples, churches, and prayer spaces in countries around the world have been devoted to spiritual meditation, learning, and growth. These estates have gardens and buildings that are deliberately designed to encourage introspection and spiritual thought. Within a church courtyard in Atlanta, Georgia, I noticed that the pathways of the garden formed a Celtic cross. Monasteries, churches, and spiritual centers deliberately cultivate an attitude of reverence and purpose in their surroundings in order to encourage people to reflect these characteristics on the inside. Despite the differences in beliefs, each sacred place has the same set of characteristics:

- ◆ Clean lines to minimize distractions.
- ◆ Cleanliness applies to the grounds, the buildings, and the people.
- ◆ The five senses are used to reinforce a feeling of calm and safety.
- ◆ Everything is chosen to deliberately create an attitude of reverence and purpose.

As a divine dreamer, your bedroom or sleeping area should reflect the same care and sense of purpose that has proved effective for seeking the Divine in culture and history. Very few people can build extensive meditation gardens, and most people live hectic lives that make major renovation of the bedroom impractical, but the ideas behind the sacred sites of the world can still be applied to your sacred rooms.

Clean lines to minimize distractions

Your mind is very impressionable and the items that surround you influence your thoughts. Bookshelves that are overstuffed and overflowing or cluttered dresser tops can be distracting to the sacred task of remembering your dreams. Each area of your bedroom, as far as it is practical, should give you a sense of pleasure and peace. This is a place that you want to see at the end of the day, not a place that reminds you of incomplete tasks and worries. Some dreamers even agree that no negative thoughts or emotions will be expressed while in the bedroom. Clean off the tops of dressers and straighten your bookshelves. Make this a place that appeals to the dreamer within.

An important quality (sometimes ignored) of sacred space is that utilitarian facilities should be understated. If you use your sleeping space for other tasks, such as for crafts or for office work, keep those areas distinct with a room divider or a piece of lightweight cloth hung from the ceiling. Desks and electronic devices, while incredibly useful for the techno-savvy dreamer, can be a distraction when first waking up. If these are important items in your bedroom, or your dream journal works best on the computer, make this space as inviting and calm as the remainder of the bedroom. Nothing is more enticing than the possibility of open workspace. This will help prevent areas that demand energy from flowing over into the peaceful area of the dreamer.

In your efforts to de-clutter the bedroom, don't forget to look at the walls and floor. These areas can provide distractions in the form of artwork and clutter (laundry and such) that you don't need as you move through the first moments of remembering a dream.

Cleanliness applies to the grounds, the buildings, and the people

Cleanliness can be as simple as putting clothes in the hamper, or as impressive as a full force Spring cleaning. The level of clean depends on you. If you suffer from allergies, dusting and vacuuming will probably give you a measure of physical comfort during sleep. (Confine this kind of cleaning to earlier in the day, however, so that the dust that stirs into the air will have time to settle before bedtime.)

The 5 senses are used to reinforce a sense of calm and safety

Seeing, tasting, smelling, touching, and hearing are our windows to the world. Through these five avenues we gain almost every piece of information we know. Within the sacred dream space of your bedroom you can influence the kinds of things your senses receive. You have power over your environment—so use it!

Visual information is the first impression you will have when you awake, so keep your artwork simple, soothing, and free of words. The human mind tries to make sense from patterns and letters, even if they are seen only for a second or they are nonsense. Eliminating words and strong patterns (as well as clutter around the room) will keep your mind focused on dream patterns. If you choose to decorate your bedroom, choose colors for the walls, drapery, and linens that are calming and inviting.

Smell (the sense that is wired directly to the side of your brain that controls your instinct) connects you to emotions and people that you can remember in no other way. Go beyond the basic idea of fresh air (a good place to begin) and choose a scent that is pleasing, calming, and enjoyable for your dream space. Many herb shops and nature stores carry scented oils and perfumes, but don't let your nose be limited to prepared scents. Explore your world using the nose, but be careful not to overwhelm your space.

The senses of *taste* and smell are closely linked (people with a strong sense of smell tend to have very sensitive taste buds), and if you appeal to one, you could very well appeal to the other. Enchiladas before bedtime may seem like a wonderful idea, but the lingering taste of acids in the mouth can be a negative influence on the sleeping mind. Vanilla is a comforting smell and can remind you of the taste of chocolate chip cookies; good if you have some on-hand, but bad if you are trying to lose weight and wake up late at night needing a snack.

Appealing to the sense of *touch* is probably the easiest. Your skin will touch sheets, pillows, comforters, pajamas, and other skin. Check to see that each of these items is appealing. Familiar old pajamas may be comforting, but if the seams are rough, they may literally be a pain in the side for your dreaming.

Last but not least is the sense of *hearing*. Some dreamers use tapes of music, drumming, chants, or Nature sounds to encourage dreaming. Other dreamers have used a small table-top water fountain on their bedside table while other dreamers prefer silence. Examine your patterns throughout the day—at work, in nature, while listening to music—and make note of the sounds that are pleasing without being distracting to your thoughts.

The items that are present on sacred sites have a specific purpose

Often, dreamers have mentioned that setting aside a special place for working on their dreams has been enough to open the gates to the dreamscape. Sometimes, though, specific pieces of art or color have been added to encourage dreams. Choose items to add to your space carefully. A blue piece of cotton cloth may encourage calmness, but it could also add the ocean's width and breadth to your dreams. Consider including statues, figurines, pictures of family members who also dream, or even a tapestry on the wall or ceiling.

Dream Pillow

Although there are many different kinds of dream pillows, I designed this one for comfort and ease of use. Smaller, more specific dream pillows can be made for special occasions when you are seeking dreams about creativity, stress, insight, personal growth, and so on. If you find that sleeping with a dream pillow is distracting or uncomfortable, try placing it on your dream altar during the night instead. You can also use it as a form of aromatherapy during your meditation or bedtime ritual or while interpreting your dreams. Simply place the pillow nearby where the scents can help you reach your dream world.

Supplies

- 6" x 19" piece of prewashed cloth (cotton or a soft blend).
- Needle and thread (or sewing machine).
- 4 safety pins (diaper pins are also durable).
- Herbs and essential oils.

Directions

1. Fold the cloth in half lengthwise so that the pattern or "right" side of the fabric is on the inside. It will form a 3" x 19" rectangle.

2. Sew along one short and one long side approximately 1/4" from the edge. This will leave an opening on the remaining short side to stuff the pillow with herbs.

3. Turn the dream pillow cover inside out so that the stitching is inside and the fabric pattern is on the outside. You should have approximately a 2 3/4" x 18 3/4" tube.

4. In a wooden or ceramic bowl, mix the following:
   - 1/4 cup mugwort.
   - 1/3 cup lavender.

- 1/3 cup chamomile flowers.
- 1/4 cup catnip.
- 1/3 cup orange peel.
- Add a drop or two of an essential oil if you would like to add special energy, but be sparing when you use essential oils because they are sometimes overpowering for the sense of smell.

5. Use the mixture to stuff your dream pillow about 2/3 full. If there are any remaining herbs, seal them in a plastic bag and save them for refreshing your pillow later.

6. Use two fo the safety pins to secure the herbs in the dream pillow. There should be an approximately 1/3 of the tube left open for mini dream pockets.

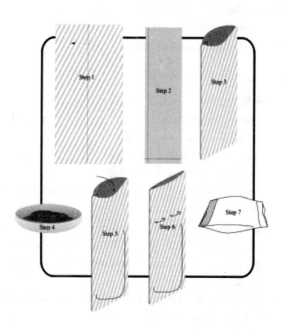

7. Use the two remaining safety pins to attach the dream pillow to the inside corners of your pillowcase. When you are lying down, the dream pillow should be close to, but not underneath, your head. As an alternative, you can pin the pillow to the fitted sheet at the head of your bed, beside your pillow, or on the exterior of the pillow.

For your mini dream pockets in the following chapters, use the same techniques you used for the larger dream pillow. Use a 4" square of fabric and label the outside of each mini-pillow for the type of dreams it will encourage (flying, premonitions, etc.). Fill each dream pocket and then sew or pin it shut to keep the herbs inside.

For your dream pockets try:

- Rosemary—dried or fresh (memory).
- Pine needles or evergreen needles (protection for the dreamer and his space).
- Dandelion flowers and leaves—dried (hopes and wishes).
- Hops (dream activator).
- Mugwort (dream activator).

As a wonderful touch, set your pillow on a windowsill during the full of the moon for blessings from the moon Goddess Selene. Ask for the blessings of the moon Goddess with this twist on a familiar children's rhyme:

Goddess bright, Goddess light,

Shine on my dreams tonight.

I wish I may, I wish I might

Have the dreams I wish tonight.

A Dream Altar

A dream altar is the perfect place to keep special items for focusing your dreams. The dream altar provides a very specific and focused area that is only for the dreamer and her developing relationship with the Goddess. This is a great compromise if you share sleeping quarters with someone and making the entire room sacred space is not practical.

Be it a window ledge, a box top, a bookshelf, a shelf hung on the wall, or the end of a dresser, it is best if your dream altar is close to the bed. Your altar will be where you will focus your energy before going to sleep, and it will provide you with a consistent reminder of your goals and purpose for dreaming during the day.

An altar dedicated to dreaming should have items that are important to you. While some things seem fairly obvious for a dream altar (the dark blues and black of night, images of the moon and stars, journals, and dream pillows), unless the objects are significant to you, the altar will remain just a pretty decoration. The importance of an item in your thoughts and beliefs will give that symbol its power for you. Examine the suggestions that follow for your altar (and any other suggestions in the rest of this book) and measure them against your inner voice. Your personal choice is the best one.

When you first begin your dream work, your altar may contain only the glass of water from the first spell in this chapter and a candle that is lightly scented. This simple and easy altar set-up allows you to place the altar on just about any surface (unlike large and complex altars) and to keep your intent for dreaming clear and uncluttered. A strong and simple symbol (such as a bundle of rosemary or maybe an old piece of memory from a computer) can be added to encourage remembering your dreams. As time and your dreaming continue, you might want to add some of the following items to your dream altar as they become appropriate for your goals:

- A cloth in dark blue (night sky) or white (sacred as purifying color to the ancients).
- Herbs from the dream pillow in a small pile as an offering to the Goddess.
- A feather to lightly trace your dream steps.
- Pictures, cutouts, or figurines that include the stars and moon and/or the Goddess.
- Peaceful incense (less likely to start a fire than a candle).
- Objects that represent your dreaming goal (soccer ball for success in games, chess piece for logic and planning, Mardi Gras beads for fun and exuberance).
- Your dream journal/tape recorder.
- Picture or representation of a door or window (as a passageway to the Goddess).
- A key (symbolic of you having the key to unlock dreams for yourself).

Journal

Personal obstacles

In the space that follows, take a moment to list your own reasons for not dreaming or remembering your dreams on a regular basis. Do you lack time? Do you wait to feel the magick of dreaming in order to work on it? Do you need/want support from others? Are you too tired in the morning? Whatever ideas come to mind, jot them down. Don't worry about structure or form.

A not-so-quick fix

Using your answers to the previous journal prompt, summarize each separate objection in a word or phrase. If "I am rushed in the morning" is one of your answers, then "time" is probably what you lack. Do you consistently lack time, confidence, or something else? Make a note of any patterns you see in your own objections. Are the things you have listed habits that are internal to you? Are these things external (job or family)? Number your objections in the order you plan to deal with them. Use only one number per obstacle. For each obstacle you should list one or two practical ideas for addressing the problem (for example, if time is one of your objections, make a plan to find 15 minutes during the day to work on dreams or wake up 10 minutes earlier).

Keep your destination in sight

Remember that your dreams are a source of energy. In the following space, list the benefits you desire from dreaming. What will you do with the energy? Finish an old project? Improve your perspective on decisions? Find your spiritual path? Weave the Goddess into your daily life? Remeber a dream each morning? Here's a hint for improving your recall: a touch of fragrance on your journal will strengthen the connection between the dreamscape and your journal.

Four
All the World's a Stage

"Dreaming is a form of thinking experienced as action."

—Richard M. Jones

The art of dreaming

Have you ever dreamed of being an artist or of writing the great American novel? Writing, painting, sculpting, programming computers, problem-solving, teaching children, and navigating the world of interpersonal relationships are all endeavors that can be seen as a kind of creativity. Dreams, with their complete freedom from the rules of reality, can be another very intense form of expression: your own art.

If you ask an artist, they will likely tell you that their art is a collaboration between their hearts and the world around them. The materials and subject of any work of art express some part of the artist and some part of his vision of the world. Some artists will also speak of a "spark," a warm and inspiring Spirit or the power of the Divine that can touch their artwork. That divine touch is often the gentle, nurturing hand of the Goddess encouraging Her children. Intense, powerful, and often simple art has resulted from the delicate balance of man and the Divine.

These artistic elements meet in a studio for you, the dream artist, known as the theatre of the mind. In this theatre, where there is an attentive audience of one, nightly shows are performed to share, enlighten, and inspire. The material for these dream plays comes from the same three-part source material used by every other artist: the Self, the Universal energy, and the Goddess (or divine source). These three pieces combine in varying proportions to create the props on stage, the curtain, the actors, the stagehands, and the director. Let's explore your mind's dream theatre and discover how you, the Universe, and the Goddess can influence your dreamscape.

The Self

Whether you subscribe to the theory of creationists, to the theory of evolution, or to another explanation of the beginning of the world, there is no doubt that each person forms a unique path in the world. No matter how many times you walk down a garden pathway (a great way to relax before dreaming), you can never walk the path the same way twice. Time, weather, and natural variety will keep it fresh and new in a myriad of large and small ways. Even the wonder of twins cannot create two people who are completely identical because the everyday experiences and interactions will make them different.

You provide the basic material for all of the images and concepts in your dream plays. Your experience gives you an additional layer of meaning for symbols that other people can't have because they're not you. A cup of coffee, for you, may mean comfort and good times with friends, while someone else will remember their work in a diner and cringe. Only you, the dreamer, can provide the correct connotations for that coffee cup. Your dreams are tailored to you by the use of symbols, which have meaning for you and not the world in general. Each experience, sight, and sound in your life can be used as symbolic language by the Goddess to spell out her love, caring, advice, and insights in symbolic words only you can understand.

This individuality is especially important to remember when you share dreams with other people and they attempt to interpret the symbolism. Sharing the dream is wonderful, and interpretations by friends are often close, but they do not have your frame of reference. Your best friend is probably trying to be helpful, but trust your own ideas first.

Symbols that might originate from the Self in dreams:
- Images from childhood events.
- Familiar people; family and friends.
- Work or school images specific to you.
- Natural images from your geographic location.
- Favorite items or experiences.

Meditation

Many of the experiences you have every day pass unnoticed because of the hectic pace of your schedule. This meditation is one method to concentrate on the world around you and your experiences. Understanding these elements of your life will begin to clarify the symbols that might be used by the Goddess in your dreams to communicate with you.

At the beginning of a regular day, close your eyes and take a few breaths. Concentrate lightly on your senses one at a time. Spend a moment identifying both the sensations and your reactions to them. (If you smell flowers, are you happy with Spring or tense about upcoming allergies?) Look around you at the ceiling, floor, and the surfaces of things near you. Continue noticing the world around you as if you are a newborn baby looking for the first time. Notice the play of light and the rich colors, the sounds that are obvious and subtle. These are the symbols and "words" that you contribute to your dreams. These are the images that have specific meaning for you. Close your eyes again. What images and sensations remain most clearly in your mind? What emotions or thoughts do you have about these images? Breathe deeply a few more times and end your formal meditation. Throughout your day, try to make note of the sensations, feelings, and images that surround you. As you notice more of your daily life, you will enrich the language between you and the Goddess. Use some of the journal space at the end of the chapter to write down the strongest thoughts and ideas.

The Universal energy

Like a ripple on the water, each action moves the world directly around you and then the wave continues outward to affect other areas. The connections between you and the other pieces of the Universe can be visualized as a web of blue light. If a thin line of blue light connects every person in the world, then you are a point on the web where several lines come together. Along these lines the energy of the Universe moves in waves to give you new experiences and to push you toward situations that can add to your life experience.

All around the world, at every time of the day, there are people living, caring, growing, dying, and changing. Each of these events, and even the smile that brightens someone's day, can send a ripple along the web of the Universe. These events outside of your direct experience are part of your unconscious experiences and can become images in your dreams. Remember as you move through your day that you are connected to everything around you, and as a point on the web you have the power to influence multiple connections through your energy. Maybe you can't change the entire Universe, but you definitely have power over your corner of it! Your smiles and frowns are the possible dream images for people around you.

It is important to remember that the Universe also has a connection to you. The power that moves the stars along their path is the same energy that keeps your heart beating. The Universal energy (understood by Carl Jung as the collective unconscious) contributes eons of knowledge and life to your dream symbols. These images are not always apparent, however, because they begin in the subconscious. Bringing them to the forefront of your dreams requires looking at the broader world around you and understanding what each symbol (stars, cities, oceans, etc.) might mean in the Universe. These are the symbols that form the background of your dream stage.

Symbols that originate from the Universe in dreams are:

- Stars or constellations.
- Compass images or "steering by the stars."
- Natural Elements (Earth, Air, Fire, Water, wood, metal, etc.).
- Large scale changes (future, past, new Universe).
- History of man scenes (from mankind's collective memory).

The Goddess

The energy of the Universe and the imagery of the Self don't begin to take form or have purpose until they are touched by the original creative force of the Goddess. It is the Goddess who says what the dream will be "about." They can be "about" love, hope, loss, or any aspect that concerns you. The Goddess is the director who encourages the set designers to shock you and helps the actors to combine elements from a tragedy and a comedy. Looking closely at which props or costumes appear on your dream stage can reveal the influence of the Goddess. If you would expect your friend to be dressed in jeans but he's wearing a tuxedo, the Goddess is probably influencing this image in your dream.

It is important, however, that you watch carefully for the imagery of the Goddess. She is part of the Universe and She is part of you. Her influence will often be subtle touches within the overall imagery of your dream. Perhaps you have the same dream, over and over, of falling and then waking before you land. This common dream can be uncommon with the influence of the Goddess. The places wehre you fall, the scenes and colors surrounding you, and even the time in your life when you dream of falling can indicate a symbolic message from the Goddess. The clearest sign that your dreams have been strongly influenced by the Goddess is your own feeling about the dream. If you feel that a dream is significant, then it is important for you.

Symbols that originate from the Goddess in dreams are:
- References to religious or sacred space or time.
- Themes of comfort and safety.
- The Cycle of Life: birth, death, and rebirth.
- Feminine creative force.
- Specific images related to specific faces of the Goddess.

The Goddess visits

Sometimes the Goddess touches your dream more strongly than others', and not always with Her choice of props. Whether the Venus of Willendorf appears as the rolling hills nearby or the Virgin Mary appears as a flowering white lily, the effect is the same. The Goddess energy has been presented in your dream to make a statement, to reach out and make sure that you are acknowledging that connection. It's her way of getting your attention. "Listen Up!" she says. Looking for signs and emblems of the Goddess is personal work, so remember to listen carefully to your intuition and be open to possibilities.

Ancient Egyptians and the early Hebrews spoke of the divine Gods and Goddesses standing at the head of the dreamer. The Goddess would give dreams in answer to the question or problem presented by the dreamer, a sure sign of the power of the Divine touching the dream world. Sometimes these dreams included symbolic visions of the Goddess (her companions or animal forms) and sometimes the Goddess herself appeared within the dream. The timing of these visits is impossible to predict (and they are rare), but a rich dreaming life that is open to possibilities is an ace up your sleeve for noticing when the Goddess makes a cameo appearance. Remembering, honoring, and studying dreams will encourage the respect and openness needed to recognize the influence of the Goddess in dreams.

The Goddess, in Her many aspects, can bring different messages, gifts, and insights to your dreams. Each Goddess brings Her own symbols and idiosyncrasies into your dreams. A strangely placed object, a woman speaking words of wisdom, or the seashore can remind you in tiny ways that the Goddess is present and available. It is this daily contact, like the chitchat of a close friend, that encourages intimacy and closeness with the Goddess.

What follows is a list of imagery, actions, and feelings that might be associated with a Goddess in your dreams. This list also includes some of the Goddess archetypes and traditional ways of representing these archetypes. The list is very abbreviated, but will provide a starting point for your own thoughts about Goddess archetypes. Listen to your own intuition and the nuances of your dreams to tell you the truth.

- Mother.
- Maiden.

- Crone.
- Earth Mother.
- Caretaker.
- Teacher/wise woman.
- Child.
- Wild woman.

Broad images that could represent the Goddess are:

- A vase or vessel that holds water that seems unusual or catches your attention.
- A woman with wisdom and insight that is unexpected or unexplained.
- Images of Earth and land that evoke a reaction of calm, soothing, or "home."
- Items of silver or rose quartz.
- Statuaries, figurines, and fountains that are particularly well carved, out of place, or resemble you or someone you know.
- A person (generally female) that you interact with in the dream as though you are close friends, but in reality you do not know this person.
- Images that resemble figurines or carvings of goddesses you know (for example, during a dream there is a picture in your home that includes the Lady of Guadeloupe).
- Bodies of water: lakes, rivers, streams, rain, and the ocean.
- Female animal images (doe, mother bear, etc.).
- Caves or underground tunnels, hills, and valleys in a landscape; fertile fields.
- The moon in its many phases, including the dark of the moon or absence of moonlight.

Each face of the Goddess carries its own personality and its own set of symbols. The Appendix of this book contains dream symbols and some of the more prominent goddesses from Celtic, Norse, Santeria, E'fa, and European cultures listed with their traditional symbols and some spiritual interpretations of these symbols when they appear in your dreams.

Variety in dreams

The Goddess and the Universe bring your dream plays to a new level by combining your symbolic language in infinitely new patterns. Even a dream that is played nightly on your stage for a week will vary in small, almost unnoticeable ways. A play can vary wildly from night to night with the energy of the actors, forgotten lines, and missed cues. These same variations occur in your dream plays, and noticing these will let you see clearly the input of the Universe, the Goddess, and yourself. They bring not only knowledge of the past and present to your dreams, but the pattern that can become the future.

If dreams were a one-man show, they would never contain anything unexpected, unusual, or new. The images and ideas would simply be a retelling of your own feelings and experiences. While this kind of dreaming would allow you to visit experiences to learn about yourself, it would not allow you to learn lessons or gain insight on a larger scale.

Combining the imagery of your Life and Universal energy can bring your dreams to a second level of dream understanding. The second level of dreams broadens your perspective to include others around you, society, smaller trends in the world around you, and action and reaction patterns of thought. The gifts of the Goddess can bring you to a third and higher level of understanding where your dreams take their messages beyond the conscious mind. It is on this third tier that you can learn your purpose for tomorrow, pieces of the plan that guide your life and insight into how it all fits together for you.

*"An uninterpreted dream is like an
unopened letter from God."*

—the Talmud

Properties management

As with most things, you must start with the basics. You should begin by identifying the symbols in your dreams and "translating" the symbolic language of the dream into something that applies to your day-to-day life. While the dream interpretations done by many psychologists leave out the influence of the Goddess, they include the powerful imagery from both you and the Universe. These are the first key pieces of the puzzle for figuring out what a dream means for you and the best place to begin understanding your dreams.

Mimes and minimalists use empty space as their tools to communicate and evoke emotion for the audience, but in your dream plays, the props, furniture, costuming, lighting, and wordplay are used to get messages across. Make no mistake, everything has a purpose and meaning in your dreams. The object may be designed to create a familiar atmosphere, but even "mood lighting" has a purpose. Just because an object doesn't jump out and shout, "Hello, I'm Divine," doesn't mean it should be ignored. If you focus entirely on the overall play and pay no attention to the smaller items within a dream, then you ignore the first avenue of communication between yourself and the Goddess symbolism. It might be that the unusual lady in the doctor's waiting room wears an image of Brigid (who specialized in healing of the eyes), and talking with her might give you ideas about why your vision is blurry.

Your job is to notice and remember the props that are used on your dream stage. The props for an average play will include everything from a pair of horn-rimmed glasses to a niche in the wall for a sconce used in scene 2. Within the dream, consider the pieces you remember. Is someone holding a particularly expensive glass while standing in a shabby apartment? Did someone smile, frown, or become preoccupied? If you recognize "your cat," but he has stripes instead of being black, then you have an important detail. These details (as many as you can remember) should be recorded in your dream journal. Even if you only remember one object, and not an entire dream sequence, record the object, your feelings, and ideas about it and the symbolism that immediately comes to mind. Sometimes in the process of recording this snippet of information you will recall other pieces. While the helpful hints and suggestions from Chapter 1 always apply to recording your dreams, focal points will add important layers of information to your dreams.

> *"He who has learned aright about the signs that come in sleep will find that they have an important influence over all things."*

—Hippocrates

A focal point

The best way to find a focal point for your dream is to ask what two or three things are most important to the dream (a bicycle, a piece of furniture, a person, a place, or an action such as getting married). Finding the object(s) and strong actions in a dream that stand out will allow you to create an outline, or skeleton, for the dream. These pieces aren't the whole picture, but they are the anchor points to which the rest of the dream will attach. One good technique for finding the central focal point for a dream is to give your dream a title. Sometimes condensing the dream to a few catchy words will force you to recognize the main piece of your dream.

Here is a list of suggestions for enriching your journal entry with details:

- Jot down key words and phrases (polka dots, well-worn shoes, color) rather than complete sentences.

- ◆ Note and consider your perspective on the object: Do you normally see it from this angle, in this place?
- ◆ Do you have an emotional reaction to the object, its placement or one of its characteristics (it's dirty and you are disgusted)?
- ◆ Note the color, pattern, texture, and size of your focal object compared to real-life objects.

Recording these important details may be the hardest part of dreaming. You may see these objects every day, but within a dream they should be rediscovered. Absolutely everything that is in a dream has a purpose or design and finds its origins within the dreamer, the Goddess, or the patterns of the Universe. The deliberate nature of these objects will make them stand out and "feel important." This is something that makes them easy to recognize but difficult to explain.

K'La's dream

I happened upon the house and decided to stop in. It was being totally remodeled. I was with another person; a man who'd gone somewhat mad due to something related to the house. I was torn between a feeling of happiness that this beautiful old house was being restored, and a feeling of loss that it would never be the same again. There were workers still working on one of the rooms. I couldn't feel the sense of haunting that I'd always felt in the house before, so I ran upstairs to the room I knew to be the most haunted. No one stopped me. I ran into the room, which had already been completely refurbished. I could begin to feel the haunting, though, and I felt a sense of elation that it was still there, that all the renovations hadn't stripped it from the house. I embraced it, and ran back downstairs. The workers asked my companion what he had stolen. I was offended because they asked strictly based on his mental state. He looked at them proudly and said, "Just this," and held up what looked like an oxygen tank. That particular item had been a part of his original breakdown. It was like he was reclaiming it, and by doing so, he could restore his shattered psyche.

Focal points within this dream might include the house, the haunted feeling, and the people. All of the other ideas within the dream (emotions about the remodeling, smaller room, interaction with the workers) are details related to greater focal points.

Here are some qualities of focal points that might help you identify them within a dream:

- High emotion in reaction to the item (positive or negative).
- Distinct appearance, color, focus, and brightness (lighting and costuming).
- Your inner voice, or instinct, seems to make something important, even if you have trouble remembering what the detail is (you know there was something on the desk, but don't recall details).
- Repetition of an object or type of object within an individual dream and from night to night.
- Symbols and representations of the Goddess.

Although the images used in dreams originate from the experiences and knowledge stored in your mind, the choice of one item over another in a specific dream is made by the Universe and the Goddess. In the artwork of your dream play, the Universe provides a broad pattern and the Goddess provides the personal touch to make your drama come alive. On the blank stage of your dreams, the Goddess is deliberately placing coffee stains on important documents to make a point (perhaps you are distracted, not treating your "real" work with enough care, or you need some help seeing the larger patterns in your task).

The imagery that is used in your dreams is an intricate combination of yourself and your daily life, the energy of the Universe, and the Goddess. The more concerned you are with your everyday life, the more that emphasis and concern will carry through to your dreams. You can enhance your ability to dream with the Goddess by focusing on Her. Meditate in front of your dream or Goddess altar. Read about famous women or Goddesses from a variety of cultures. These actions will bring the spiritual goal of your dreaming into focus.

Capturing the dream

The written language has only been around for a few thousand years, but cave dwellers began using the natural materials around them to fashion images and artwork of their world 35,000 years ago. Art is the result of someone's perspective and one of the oldest forms of communication. It is sometimes easier to show than to tell. Dreams look and feel three-dimensional and it is likely that you will need to use a variety of expressive forms to capture the essence of a dream. In addition to the traditional written version of a dream add a bit of drawing, references to pop culture, quotes from lyrics, and use some colored pencils. Some dreamers even keep old newspapers handy and add those elements to their dream journals.

You should include drawings and visual references for the dreams you record in this chapter. This is the beginning of a process of putting the importance of dreaming over the need to "perform." You are not drawing for a contest or a teacher; you are simply putting your ideas on paper for your own reference. Give your internal critic a cup of coffee and send him on break. Once the critic is gone, use whatever method is available that feels right. If you have trouble with the idea of drawing, cut images from magazines, junk mail (a great recycling idea), or old wrapping paper.

*"The first thing, then in this non-interpretive approach to
the dream is that we give time and patience to it, jumping to
no conclusions, fixing it in no solutions. Befriending the
dream begins with a plain attempt to listen to the dream, to
set down on paper or in a dream diary in its own
words just what it says. ...and so one takes care receiving the
dream's feelings, as with a living person with whom
we begin a relationship."*

—James Hillman

Journal

Dream Pocket

Every person has a creative side, whether it is painting, writing, or solving problems in the computer world. Encourage your creative side by using a solid color fabric for your dream pocket and decorating the pocket to encourage dreams with vivid imagery.

For your dream pocket try:

- ◆ Rose petals (inspiration).
- ◆ Violet petals (creativity).
- ◆ Clear sage or geranium leaves—dried (to avoid nightmares).
- ◆ Hazelnuts or hazelnut oil (insight and resolution).
- ◆ Grapevine or ivy (career or pathwork).

Finding a focal point

Using either your journal from Chapter 1 or your past dreams, identify (underline or circle) the focal points in two or three dreams. Remember as you begin to identify the focal points or main "props" in your dreams that this is only the beginning of a process for understanding and internalizing your dreams. Attempting to make a complte picture out of these pieces is as futile as trying to imagine the Sistine Chapel's ceiling by looking at the colors Michaelangelo used. Relax and take it one dream a time. List these focal points and take a moment to speculate on what each one might symbolize for you.

The next step

Record several nights of dreams and identify the focal points in these dreams as well. Next, list the focal points from your dream separately and begin looking at their possible symbolism and emotional connection.

- Are these items from your past, present, or maybe the future?
- Do you recognize all of the people?
- What association might modern society attach to the focal point? (house is stability, home, happiness, family, responsibility, etc.)
- What association might modern psychiatry have for this focal point? (the house represents the Self.)
- What emotions did you experience in the dream overall? At what particular points?
- Were there any events or items that were surprising or unusual in the dream?
- When you think of each focal point, what is the next idea, image, or thought that occurs to you?

Five
Layers Within Dreams

The gentle language of flowers has been examined and expressed for centuries, but what these natural beauties say to our hearts has yet to be captured in one definition. Stems, leaves, thorns, and fluttered petals combine to form a mystique that captures the imagination and leads your mind to imagine other worlds. Dreams are your roses from the night. Gently they rest and await picking. Each petal and thorn is a subject to be examined. But the language of the dream is like that of the rose: not to be taken apart in too much detail. The details and symbols within dreams only give you small pieces of the whole. Just as the leaves are not the whole rose, the individual symbols and their "interpretations" are not the entirety of a dream's meaning.

Details within a dream aren't useless, however, and they will help you begin to piece together the message of your dream. Dream interpretations in the past have focused almost entirely on one or the other of two methods for interpretation: symbols by themselves or the gestalt (overall idea) of a dream. The answer is not found in either interpretation, but rather in something else that combines the two perspectives.

*"Dreams say what they mean, but they don't say it
in daytime language."*

—Gail Godwin

The language of symbols

Symbols, simply put, are anything that can represent something else, and they can have multiple meanings. Perhaps you found a rocking chair as one of the focal points within your dream. Your rocking chair can be interpreted using personal symbolism (the chair represents comfort from childhood), cultural symbolism (patience, rest), and subconscious symbolism (elderly, inactive). How these meanings relate to your dream is a choice only you can make using your intuition.

In order to consider as many of the interpretations as possible, it will be helpful for you to know what layers of symbolism are available. Imagine that your dream is a basic line drawing on a plain white piece of paper. Over this outline you are able to place transparent sheets (individual layers of symbolism) that contain colors in a certain palate: red, orange, blue, green, etc. These colors help to further define the picture of your dream. You can use some colors but not others, exclusively shades of gray, or some combination. In the same way, you can combine some, all, or none of the layers that follow.

Psychological understanding of dream symbols

Unfortunately, choosing one meaning for individual symbols is a common mistake among the psychologists who handle dream interpretation. One of the earliest and most intense dream analysts was Sigmund Freud, the father of modern psychology. Similar to some of the theories of dream interpretation that followed, Freud believed that symbols had fixed meanings within the dream world. A dream was viewed as a symptom of illness, and each person and thing within a dream represented something specific in your life (generally related to repressed sexual desires). Freud proposed that by finding meanings for each of the symbols you could then add them up to an overall interpretation of the dream and treat the illness of the patient's mind.

Carl Jung, a student and colleague of Freud's, believed that the imagery in dreams was symbolic of the subconscious, as described by Freud, and also of the collective human unconscious (sometimes referred to as ancestral knowledge). According to Jung, the subconscious and the collective unconscious can provide practical insight into the daily life of the dreamer. Jung's theory of dream interpretation relied on a system of archetypes (mother, maiden, crone, warrior, etc.) that connect the dreamer to the entirety of human experience.

Walking on the bones of the ancestors

Grandfathers, hold my feet

To the path I must lead.

In my bones are your eyes,

Wisdom is my marrow.

Your lessons are my warnings—

To step lightly.

Grandfather, walk with me.

Most modern dreamers agree that regardless of what system you use for interpretation, the images in a dream have symbolic importance for the dreamer. Just as a detective looks for unwritten messages, you are a detective dreamer looking for the purpose and pattern within your dreams. The variety of materials available from the psychological community is impressive, but I will only briefly summarize some of the main concepts. Look at the symbols within your dream and examine the following suggestions on psychological symbolism to see if they fit your dream.

- ◆ Your dream could demonstrate a deeply held desire or fear. These emotions can be repressed or subconscious due to your own filters or societal taboos. Are you dreaming about issues, actions, or people that are uncomfortable for you in the waking world?

- ◆ The people within the dream are not separate from yourself, but in fact represent aspects of your own personality. Dreams are a way of reflecting on our own actions. What in your life could your dream be commenting on?

- ◆ The actions and the people within the dream can represent a struggle for power within your life or even over your own decisions. Does your dream accurately reflect your control in your life or your perception of your ability to control?

- ◆ Your dream places you in the same overall position (with variances in the details of the scene) in order to point out a pattern in your behavior. Look at the similarities and differences that your subconscious influenced.

"The dream, far from being the confusion of haphazard and meaningless associations it is commonly believed to be, or a result merely of somatic sensations during sleep as many authors suppose, is an autonomous and meaningful product of psychic activity."

—C. G. Jung

Body, mind, and spirit layers of meaning

Just as each symbol has a myriad of possible meanings, each dream has many layers of possible information for the spiritual seeker.

Body

"Body" symbolism within the dreamscape can apply to your physical body (comforts, aches, needs, etc.), the body of the Earth (of which you are a part), ancestral knowledge (connected to you through your body), and even your physical surroundings (office, weather, etc.). Your dreams can also reflect the influences of the modern world on your body, your personal image, and your health.

The rocking chair from our previous example would touch on the body layer of symbolism by suggesting a reclining, inactive, or passive body position. In the rocking chair, you would be removed physically from activity. The chair might also touch this layer of dream to suggest that you need to relax. The tension that remains in your muscles from your day can influence your dreams in the same way that worry can make a person sick. Your body will take the opportunity of dreams to express its needs and complaints.

Your body and its DNA provide a very concrete link to ancient people and their soft-spoken gift of ancestral knowledge. For example, people from Western Europe (Celtic ancestry) often report that they are inexplicably drawn to Celtic knotwork and modern men find that primal drumming (or the rhythms of rock and roll) answers some deep need. Art and rhythm are two ways of connecting to the uncanny, but familiar, knowledge provided by your ancestors. Consider what the body of humanity might be saying through you.

Images of natural elements or scenes within a dream that include plants and animals can address your relationship with the Earth. As part of the ecosystem contained on Earth, our bodies are integral to the cycle created by the Goddess. Our decisions (to recycle, to procreate, to cherish, to destroy) are also integral to Her cycle. Many of the Earth-focused religions draw a close connection between you, your health and happiness, and the health of the world around you. In dreams where natural images are prevalent, consider what commentary they might offer for your relationship with the natural world around you. What is the body of Nature saying through you?

Ron's dream

I was with people I didn't know when we climbed up a big structure. The structure was white with the center vertical bar being dark in color. It was around 75-100 feet tall. It was somewhat tall and looked the same on both sides. We climbed up to the top of it, and then we slid down the center of the other side that was a slide, which emptied out into a lake. I'm swimming around this small lake and I see people I know swimming in the lake as well. I swim to one corner of the lake and I go into a cave that's filled with water. The sides of the cave all have furniture, couches, and end tables…it's a furnished cave. I start to swim out of the cave, but there's a snake in the water between me and the exit. It starts swimming out of the cave, so I follow it, but not too closely. It gets cornered and the snake looks like its feeling threatened, so I back off a bit and wait for it to leave.

While there are many layers of symbolism in Ron's dream, looking specifically at the body layer can help focus his attention and give him some insights. Ron should notice three strong "body" symbols: water (a force of Nature that often represents emotions and moves him from place to place in the dream), associating with a pack (safety in numbers, an instinct), and his entry into the cave (possibly an allusion to returning to the womb).

These suggestions will help you to develop the body layer of meaning within your dreams:

- ✦ Describe the physical appearance of your dream's image or focal point.
- ✦ What Natural Elements are represented?
- ✦ Does the symbol reflect a natural cycle? (predator and prey; birth, death, and rebirth).

+ Does this symbol answer any of your body's needs for survival?
+ If the symbol is an animal, where is the animal most often found? What are some common characteristics of that animal?
+ Does the image contain symbols relating to your body?
+ Does the imagery suggest parallel ideas that relate your body and the world around you?

Mind

The mind layer of interpretation addresses the parts of a dream that are related to decisions, logic, insight, and thought. Imagery of mazes, choices, puzzles, and problems are all dreams that can strengthen your mental abilities, point out weaknesses in logic, or teach the value of finding out all the information in a situation.

You can justifiably fill years worth of dream journals just with the mind's need to evaluate and review the day's events. Dreams that review a day or an event aren't always exact, however, and the resulting dreams can be confusing. In Ron's dream, the imagery came from work, his knowledge and experience with the world, and his hobby of exploring caves. The mind layer of understanding takes these familiar elements and rearranges them to help Ron look at the changes in his world in a new way. He goes through several stages of being powerful and in control (climbing), acknowledging a change (slide), and then an uncertain balance between his own control (swimming) and the tide of things around him and larger than him (the water). The changes and unusual elements within a dream are placed there by the mind to draw your attention. The change is unexpected and gets your dreaming Self to take a closer look.

Once the ideas and feelings of your dream have been recorded in detail, you should examine your focal points for symbolism at the mind layer. Try examining your focal points using the questions that follow. The greatest gift of the mind is the ability to show you perspectives that are old, new, and unusual.

- Are you experiencing the dream as someone or something else or as yourself? Explain this perspective and your emotions toward this change within the dream.

- Were there elements of the dream that were reflections from the current day, past events, or new elements (past/future/myth/fantasy)? This is your mind trying new ideas and exploring. For each major person or element within the dream describe the difference between the dream role and the role in reality. In some dreams, the difference may not be the people, place, event, or perspective, but the relationship between these four (for example, your boss and your wife are married).

- Is this a recurring dream or a recurring theme? If so, how often does it occur and is there a pattern to the dream's appearance?

Spirit

The dreamscape lifts the veil between your spirit and the Goddess each night. Within your dreams She becomes the unknown made knowable; the insight and the "aha!" experience that allows you to grow and learn. If the body layer understanding answers "what" and the mind layer answers the "how" within dreams, the Spirit layer answers the "why."

In every dream there are elements of the spirit, but recognizing dreams that contain strong spirit influences can be a little daunting. First, you must recognize what "spirit" feels like.

You have probably found places that you can label as "spiritual" or touched by the Divine, but deciphering what makes these things powerful is difficult. There is something that seems to be added to a regular dream that gives it a special glow; in the theatrical world it would be special lighting or music. Feelings of unearthliness, an importance to the moment, hairs raising on the back of your neck, goose bumps, a strangeness, or overwhelming power are all clues to identifying a spiritual place. These are the same clues you need to recognize a spirit-filled dream.

The more your ability to listen to the Goddess grows, the more symbolism you will find in your dreams at the spirit layer. Use the following questions as a guideline when you begin to search your dreams and focal points for spirit symbolism.

- Does the dream seem to focus on issues that apply to larger themes within life? Examples of these themes include good versus evil, your purpose in life, and so on.
- Does your dream include imagery related to specific places that you have experienced as spiritual?
- Did you experience elation, joy, or a sense of connection with the Universe? A sense of openness, peace, calm, or enlightenment? A sense that the events/items in a dream are deeply significant?
- Do images of the Great Mother (chalice, Earth, stars in a night sky, bounty, etc.) or images of a specific Goddess (red for Kali; needlecraft for Brigid) appear? Any image of Divinity can be used here.
- Are there any emblems, insignias, or images that are associated with you within the dream? (I find that a flower with five petals is a natural symbol for my personal beliefs and its appearance in my

dreams tells me I am looking at my own spiritual growth.)

In order to begin recognizing the touch of spirit within dreams, you must first recognize it in the waking world. Here is an exercise to help you with this process.

Spiritual places

Find a place where you will be undisturbed for a few minutes. Ground and center your energy. When you whisper the word "spiritual," are there any images, thoughts, or colors that come to mind? Sometimes the concept of spirit is found in a place, a person, or an action. In your journal, list the places and times when you have known that you were in the presence of the Goddess or something strongly spiritual. Sometimes a moment after a rainstorm will reveal a rainbow and the beauty will touch your heart. Whatever the situation, include as much detail as possible, especially about the qualities of the experience that made it spiritual (energy or purpose of a place, the attitude and worldview of someone). Include all of your senses and any subconscious or nonrational feelings or experiences.

Window on the spiritual

Whether you are Pagan, Christian, Jewish, or Moslem, the kaleidoscope of colors in a stained glass window are breathtaking. Often these windows reflect important spiritual scenes. These steps will help you create your own spiritual window as a reminder of your personal spiritual places.

Supplies

- Old magazines, newspapers, pictures, etc. that can be torn.
- Small posterboard, foam board, or paper (suggested size 11" x 14").
- Glue, scissors, and a black marker.

Directions

1. Select a place (real or imaginary) that you feel represents spiritual energy for you. Concentrate on this image as you complete this exercise.

2. Choose an overall shape for your stained glass image that is pleasing to you (circles, squares, triangles, rectangles, or uneven edges). Using the black marker, trace only the outside edge of your "window on the spiritual" onto the posterboard. (You can also choose to let your images define the shape.)

3. Select images, colors, and words from magazines and newspapers that symbolize your spiritual place or spirituality in general for you. Tear or cut these from the magazine.

4. When you have collected several, glue them to the posterboard or paper with their edges touching or overlapping. Let the glue dry completely. Try to fill every space within your "window." Using a large black marker, trace these overlapping edges. These lines will form the "leading" within your stained glass window. You might choose to cut the "window" from its surrounding paper.

5. Hang or display this "window" where you will see it frequently. Near your bed, on your closet door, or in your kitchen are particularly good places. This project works well as a focal point on your dream altar.

Balance

The temptation for dreamers is to interpret all or none of their dreams as spiritual. In the growth of society, we have grown farther from the Earth and the Goddess, and have grown distant from an essential quality of Nature: balance. The growth of humanity has, unfortunately, dimmed the memory that each person holds a vital place in the Cycle of Life. Your dreams seek a balance between the body, mind, and spirit dreams just as the animals seek a balance in the food chain. As part of the Cycle, you are part of creation—sacred by your existence. As you interpret your dreams, strive for this kind of balance.

Layers upon layers

Once you have looked at your dream and considered the focal points from the body, mind, and spirit perspectives, there are other layers of meaning that you can add to your understanding of dreams. Most dreams contain two or more layers of meaning (after all, you are a complex human), but your dreams don't need to have every layer of meaning. Your instincts will quickly tell you whether a layer of meaning has anything to offer for a particular dream. Trust these instincts. If you dream about a horrible dentist, consider the body level of understanding (you're afraid of pain and the dentist) and ignore the layers of symbolism that seem like too much work (spiritual might be a stretch for this one).

Here are some suggestions for other types of meaningful layers that you can add to your dream interpretation:

- Instinctual associations and memories (lilies might remind you of your mother).
- References to time frame. When it happened in the dream and also whether it was a past, present, or future event, person, or thing.
- Emotional responses to individual focal points. If your dreaming reaction is different than what you would expect in waking time, you might make a note.
- Elemental associations for items. Many Earth-focused paths recognize four natural Elements

of Earth, Air, Fire, and Water with a fifth Element of Spirit. Often, the pieces of your dream can easily align with one of these Elements (trees with Earth, metal pipes with Fire, a friend's sailboat with Water, and so on). Which Elements you choose and how you assign them will depend on your personal preference and your spiritual training and path. However, when looking at a focal point to determine its Elemental association, don't make assumptions. The symbol within the dream may act like an unusual Element. (For example, a volcano is a mix of Fire and Earth: How does it act or feel within the dream?)

• Male/female dichotomy associations for focal points. Often the division of ideas and energy into the God/Goddess energies can influence your view of the world around you. For example, a person who is aggressive may be seen as male, regardless of actual gender. The roles that the Goddess and the God play in maintaining balance are important, so note these symbols over a large span of time, if possible.

• Seasonal associations for focal points. Does an item remind you of Spring, or do you always see this person in the Winter? Many of the seasonal cycles are reflected in the stories and myths of the Goddess and the God. Each year, so the European stories relate, the Goddess emerges as a young maiden in the Spring, frolics during the Summer, grows to become a mother in the Fall, and returns to the underworld in the Winter. The actual dates of these changes vary from one spiritual tradition to another, but the pattern can suggest some symbolism that could be useful for your dreams. Are you constantly dreaming of

Summer (waiting for things to come to fruition), and never quite reaching Fall (harvesting what you've worked for)?

♦ Animal totems or signs of these animals. This layer is particularly helpful for people who follow Native spiritual traditions. Particularly in North America, animals are seen as brothers and sisters to man and they lend their unique qualities and lessons to your dreams. For example, images of a mouse in your dreams might initially feel unimportant or make you think that you are "small." Understanding the nature of the mouse—to see details—can give you insight into how this totem animal helps you understand the situation and your own relationship to the events of your day.

♦ Goddess associations for your dream symbols are extremely important. While the psychology, body, and mind layers of symbolism may ignore it, your connection to Brigid's well in Ireland should not be ignored. Dreams where the colors white and blue are prevalent may suggest your connection to the African Goddess Oshun and the areas of Life she influences. Making the connection between your symbols and the Goddess can help you focus on learning a life lesson from a dream rather than resolving just the situation.

♦ Sacred numbers of items within the dream. Throughout history there have been numbers that are considered to be sacred to a spiritual path (three was sacred to the Celts and can also refer to the Threefold Law) or to a particular goddess (nine was sacred to the Valkeries).

♦ Tarot card (or rune) symbols and their alternate meanings outside of the dream. A cup may symbolize many things, but for Tarot, the suit of Cups represents the emotions, relationships, and interpersonal connections. This layer of symbolism is probably strongest for anyone who uses the Tarot regularly. Other divination systems such as the I Ching, tea leaves, and runes can also present their symbolism within the dream world.

- Religious symbols are common within dreams. Earth-based spirituality and both Pagan and ritual symbols can be a distinct layer for understanding your dreams. A sword, while a cutting instrument used for defense in reality, can be a symbol for a person's will within some spiritual traditions. The tools, rituals, and celebrations that are part of your spiritual path may become intricately woven into your dreams. This is the time when a knife is not simply a knife, it may be an athame. If you have experience with other religious paths (Christianity, Buddhism, Judaism, and so forth), then those symbols may also appear on this level.

- Active/passive participation in a dream. For each major element, determine whether it is acting within the dream or being acted upon. For example, a normal deck of cards could be passive, but in *Alice in Wonderland* they were active.

- Society gives you a number of built-in symbols that can be used in your dreams, either by themselves or in contrast with other elements. At this layer of symbolism, you might also find that all tigers are named Tony.

- Chakras are seven centers of light and spiritual energy aligned along the human spine. The seven chakras and their symbolic associations are:

1. Root: (base of spine/white light) material or physical world and needs, the power to manifest.

2. Hara: (sexual organs/purple light) giving physically.

3. Solar Plexus: (belly button/blue-violet or golden light) relationships with others, positive confrontation.

4. Heart: (over the heart/rose pink light) the ability to love everyone and everything from a divine perspective, working creatively.

5. Throat: (voice box/clear blue light) feelings of peace, strength, and security; the ability to communicate and share; and humor.

6. Third Eye: (between eyebrows/green light) clairvoyance, thinking beyond time and space, visions, premonitions.

7. Crown: (top of the head/golden yellow light) Divine understanding and wisdom.

Remember that these layers, and any others that you develop, are just layers of symbolism that can add up to a personal understanding of dreams. After two or three layers, you will often find that a dream's symbols become easy to identify as either body, mind, or spirit. The layers are very complimentary, but keeping track of several layers of symbolism can get rather crowded within your journal. In the next chapter you will explore ways to organize these layers and find the patterns between them.

Journal

Dream Pocket

As the layers of meaning become evident to you, keep your dream pocket simple and you'll prevent confusion.

For your dream pocket try:

* A drop of ylang-ylang oil on a cotton ball (intuition).
* Sandalwood incense or oil (for spiritual focus).

A sense of Self

If you ask someone on the street to describe who they are, many times the person will list their titles. Some people wear the hat of wife, mother, husband, employee, caregiver, family accountant, etc. List as many of your own titles as possible down the left side of the page. Beside each title identify the person who benefits from your efforts (for employee: boss; for caregiver: family, pets, etc.). How many of these titles define you as the person who benefits from your efforts?

After considering each of these titles, draw a line down the page and label the list you made as "outside." Now, create a list of your characteristics from the "inside": You are loving, insightful, careful, honest, etc. These are the qualities that truly describe you and not just what you do. Defining yourself by what you do can become a slippery slope that leads to losing your own identity. If you run into trouble finding these personal qualities, look at the list of titles you have on the outside. These are the results of something you are; being a caregiver is probably the result of caring, empathy, friendship, etc. These internal qualities are more likely to be the ones that you will find in dealing with spiritual dreams, rather than your everyday "titles." These will be the deeper themes and symbols within your dreams.

Personal symbols

Keep a running list of symbols and ideas that seem to repeat in your dreams. These recurring themes deserve more in-depth research and consideration than everyday themes. If you have dream journals from the past, begin your list by using symbols from those dreams. Take the time to look each item up in the dictionary in the Appendix, in another respected dream dictionary, or on the Internet. If possible, find images of these symbols and keep them for use in your dream journal. Your symbols will develop over time. The original meanings you find for a symbol are just a starting point for later meanings. As you develop and grow, as you learn lessons from life and your experiences, you can find new meanings within a symbol.

Practice with layers of meaning

Over the course of a week, record your dreams in detail. Remember to include as many of your senses and emotions as possible. For each dream, identify the focal points and relate them to the body, mind, and spirit layers of understanding. Add any of the other layers that seem important. Some focal points will be easier than others, and while one focal point may have all three layers of meaning, another focal point may only have one.

Six
The Sum of the Parts

Anyone who speaks multiple languages will tell you that interpreting concepts and ideas from one language to another is difficult because there are words and ideas in one language that don't exist in another language. In the process of translating an idea, some of the original meaning is lost or oversimplified. In the same way, the language of dreams has its own idioms and concepts that do not translate easily or completely into symbols and imagery.

Learning the language of dreams begins like learning a foreign language: You build a vocabulary of words and then develop phrases. Understanding the symbols and themes in your own dreams is the beginning of your dream vocabulary. The next step toward understanding your dream language is to step away from the details and look at the dream as a whole. Like looking at an impressionist painting, you need a little bit of perspective to gain an understanding of your dreams. Mapping your dreams, which is discussed later in this chapter, can help you gain this perspective.

"The eye sees a thing more clearly in dreams than the imagination awake."

—Leonardo da Vinci

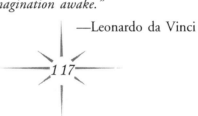

117

Perspective

Two kinds of perspective changes are necessary to look at a dream as a whole. First, you must step away from the details of the dream and look at the larger issues and themes. Second, you need to be open mentally to all of the possible messages in your dreams.

You can view your dreams from the front row of the mind's theatre (with lots of individual symbols), but the top of the curtains and even the actors will be somewhat out of focus. Your perspective is too close. When a critic goes to see a play, he doesn't sit in the front row, center seat—and neither should you! To appreciate the play of your dreams, you need to understand not only the individual symbols but also their relationship to each other. For example, cats, rats, and wiggly things might be symbols that are confusing unless seen together as pieces of a children's song that honors all living creatures. Sometimes it happens that symbols don't make sense when they are separate, but they form a clear picture when put together. One of the best ways to gain perspective on your dreams is to set the dream aside for a while. Even a few minutes away can be helpful.

In the same way that plays are created for an expectant audience, dreams are designed for you when you are centered and open to ideas. Listening only to the lead actor in a play, you miss out on the subplots and intricacies of the entire play. In order to get the most out of your dreams, you need to listen to all of the messages. Your internal critic (the one who corrects grammar, deletes "inappropriate" ideas, etc.) is the biggest obstacle at this point to your sacred dreams and the insights they contain.

Try the following meditation to aid you with concentration, energy, openness, and protection while you are reviewing your dreams.

Breathing meditation

Breathing is an easy reminder of your connection to the Earth and the Goddess. This exercise will help you establish a sacred mindset. Through a process of three breaths you can center and calm the three spheres of the Self—body, mind, and spirit.

1. Body breath: Inhale the life-giving air slowly (counting to five). This is the breath that connects and surrounds all life. Feel the air expand your lungs and imagine it filling your entire body with light. Exhale slowly and relax any muscle tension, soreness, or demands by your body, such as hunger or thirst.

2. Mind breath: Inhale slowly and visualize the oxygen flowing to your brain and increasing your awareness. Feel the strength and openness in your mind. Exhale slowly, releasing worry, responsibility, and negative thoughts as energy that can be transformed by the Universe.

3. Spirit breath: Inhale slowly and visualize your spirit filled with renewal and hope from the unending power of the Universe. You are taking in and opening your connection to the Web of Life. Exhale slowly and release your anxieties, doubts and your unanswered questions.

Use this process of calming and centering yourself whenever you begin working on your dreams or sacred path.

Free association with your dream

With your mind open, you are ready to mentally review your dream using a process called free association (developed by Freud). It is not important where you are (driving, cleaning, meditating), but it is important that you feel safe and calm.

Free association is quite simple. Clear your mind and then begin thinking about your dream. Allow your mind to generate ideas naturally, and then follow your thoughts. Even if these thoughts don't seem to make sense, they are part of your thoughts for a reason.

For example, if the tricycle in a dream leads you to think of antique toys, childhood, metal recycling for the war, veterans, and so on, then you have hit upon a symbol that is particularly rich for you. Allow yourself to follow the train of thoughts around the symbol until you start thinking: *Okay, what next?* If it helps, write down some of your thoughts in the margins of your journal. Your response to the dream might include emotions, thoughts, associations, and some "obvious" connections or ideas about the source of the dream. Learn to rely on and trust the images that occur to you after your breaths. Distractions and daydreaming can be important signs that your mind is avoiding the true topic of your dream, so pay close attention.

You might try to recreate the feeling or emotion you had during the dream. Was it fear, excitement, wonder, curiosity, or a mixture of these? If you have trouble placing a clear label on your dream, try identifying it as a positive or negative feeling. Emotions are closely linked to chemicals in your body, and recreating the emotions will help you to recreate the chemical state of your body during the dream. This "chemical dreaming" can actually help you to remember details and explore the dream.

Finding the "true" meaning

If your dream could apply to two or three situations, your instinct can help determine which situations are correct. Treat the dream as a transparency that you can lay over your situations. As the dream idea is laid over your situation, imagine yourself briefly marking the strongest points of comparison. Sit quietly and compare each scenario against the dream. You will probably find that one situation rings true and that you have to work to make the dream fit as well into other situations. Don't be fooled into trying to seek the "right" or "correct" dream interpretation.

Finding the best interpretation when there are several possibilities is both important and tricky. The same signals that indicate someone might be lying are the signals you will likely receive when you are ignoring your own instincts for what is the best match for your dream:

- Physical reaction while examining the dream: Increased heart rate, heart skips a beat, nervous or anxious, goose bumps, the hair on your arms stands up. These are signs that this is an emotional connection for you. Take the hint.

- Hyperfocus: When you look at the scenarios, one of them may seem brighter, more focused, or appear as a clearer image than the other two. This additional "focus" is your mind's eye making more points of correspondence than you are consciously making on your own.

- Automatic or assumed dismissal of an idea: If you dismiss an idea because "it is just too long ago," or "that can't be it," then you should re-examine that concept. Often dreamers dismiss entire conversations with the Goddess based solely on the idea that it was "unlikely."

- Second guessing: If you are still vaguely uneasy or have doubts once you have made your choice, then you probably have not chosen the best interpretation.

It is possible that your dream can apply to more than one situation at once, just as it can have symbolism from many layers of understanding. Layers of symbolism and a new perspective can help you choose the *best* interpretation, not the *only* one. If you find that two situations seem to be equally applicable to the dream, consider the idea that your dreamscape could either be commenting on both situations individually or drawing parallels between them. This kind of dual purpose dreaming is extremely helpful because it not only lines up the two situations to be viewed against the dream, but also against each other.

Once you review your dreams and any possible and obvious interpretations, you may find that none of your ideas quite fit the dream. This is a perfect time to relax, let the possibilities of the dreamscape open within your mind, and release the need to assign the dream a firm meaning. The language of dreams sometimes gives you a clear message and sometimes it does not. You may need to gain experiences, grow personally, or progress spiritually before the deepest understanding of these dreams will be available to you. Or, you may find that worry, fatigue, or larger events in your life cloud your reception of the message.

Mapping your dream

For dreams that defy interpretation or for a dream that you truly want to explore in depth, you may want to try several different approaches for understanding. Aside from identifying focal points, finding symbolism, and viewing dreams from an overall perspective, you can try making a "map" of your dream. Mapping is a brainstorming technique that has been used successfully by psychologists, teachers, and corporate managers. Mapping is a technique that is used to express and examine the relationship between individual pieces of a puzzle, and those individual pieces and the whole. Some dreamers find that free association without paper and pen allows them more freedom, but for dreamers who easily forget, or who prefer to visually "lay it all out," mapping can be an excellent tool.

You will work with the ideas in your dreams and sketch their relationships, rather than just drawing a picture of a place in your dream. Around each item on the map you can add information you know: symbolic layers of meaning, spiritual connotations, and associations. You can also link different items and look at similar elements or their differences.

Ricky's dream will serve as an example as you work with the mapping technique.

Ricky's dream: "The Graveyard"

I am in a car going into a graveyard and there is a big hole in my way with metal poles sticking out of it. I think to myself, *I can't do that.* Then, I decide to walk over the hole and nothing happens. Off to my left there are cheerleaders that I don't recognize. I go into the graveyard. Then I am walking along stepping-stones coming into the graveyard from another direction. I meet Dawn and she says something to me (I can't remember) and I go along the pathway. I also see Gareth.

In the first attempt to process this dream, Ricky drew a map of the dream's location. This helped him to establish a basic idea of what elements were where and a sequence of events. For dreams that have a definite location, drawing the location is helpful, even if you think it is just a place you normally go. In Ricky's dream, the graveyard looked normal, but drawing the map helped him discover that the graveyard was on the opposite side of the road from its real-life position. Following are the basic steps you can use to map your dream:

1. Identify the dream you are mapping by its title, date, or the page in your journal (Ricky: "The weird Graveyard dream," early to mid-October).

2. Your most important focal point (Ricky: graveyard) will be in the center of your "map" as a first or A-level focal point. You can change the focal point to be less important if you discover another aspect of the dream gives you more developed

concepts and thoughts. Draw a circle around the word or phrase. This will form the "axle" for the rest of the information. Short descriptive words, key phrases, and abbreviations work well for mapping.

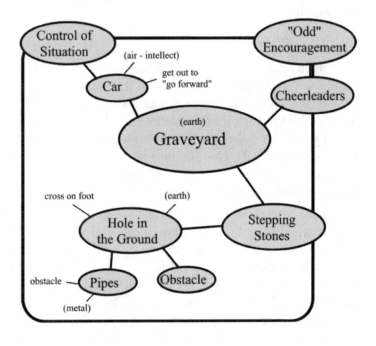

3. Select three or four focal points that seem to represent the major categories, sections, or ideas within the dream and place them around the first circle (see diagram above). Each of these second-level focal points (B-level) should also be enclosed in a circle. If several items within your dream can be grouped under a category (people, office details, a room, etc.), then it may be helpful to use the category for the B-level rather than individual descriptions. (Ricky:

"Gareth," "Dawn," and "cheerleaders" could have been grouped as "people.")

4. Begin including specific details for both A and B focal points. These details will look similar to spokes around the focal point circles (see diagram on page 124). Sometimes a focal point will suggest many details, and sometimes only a few. Some helpful things to include about a focal point are discussed in Chapter 5. You might also want to include some spatial relationships between the symbols in the dream.

5. Include the function of the different elements within your dream. Just as a story has an antagonist, protagonist, and conflict, a dream has characters and events. Does each piece of the dream help you on your pathway within the dream? Does it present an obstacle, a tool, or someone who is familiar or unfamiliar? These contributions may not be obvious, so look for lessons in hidden places (a friend is cast as the antagonist, etc.). (Ricky: The hole was an obstacle, the stepping-stones and cheerleaders were helping him toward his goal, and seeing Gareth was neutral.) Do the unrelated pieces of the dream share an element (for example, they are all tools, excuses, people in positions of power, places of spiritual energy, etc.)? Does one element require the others to work?

6. Completing your map is subjective. You will know that it is done when all of the essential pieces are on the map (not all of the details need to be on the map, just the important ones) and you feel like the map represents the essence of the dream. As is the case with layers of symbolism, however, your map isn't complete without

some perspective. After a few cleansing breaths, look at your dream map with new eyes and add any information that occurs to you.

7. Review the importance of your focal points. Sometimes focal points lead you to explore an area that is completely different from what you expect. Don't be distressed or surprised if a secondary piece of your map seems to belong in the center when you are done. Associations are complex and can surprise you. (Ricky: The hole in the ground was secondary on the map but ended up being central to understanding the message of the dream.)

8. Even daily issues within dreams can reflect the three major themes in dreams. These universal struggles are the same ones that have given strength and appeal to the literature of nearly every culture on Earth: man vs. man; man vs. Nature; and man vs. God or Goddess. Look within your map for these universal themes. Not all dreams focus on these universal themes, but most do. (Ricky: He finds his personal pathway in the world—a struggle with himself for control (man vs. man) and with Nature/Universe for the pathway that is correct for him.)

As with art and literature, dreams have their own structure and meaning. Ricky noticed that he was going somewhere (motivation) and that the hole was an obstacle to his progress. At first he did not go over it because he believed he couldn't, but he made the conscious decision to proceed anyway. Ricky looked at the function of each item within the dream rather than at what the items actually were. In his dream it was his conscious decision to go forward over a perceived difficulty (the hole wasn't really a hole) that helped him reach his goal.

Missing elements

"It is in our idleness, in our dreams, that the submerged truth sometimes comes to the top."

—Virginia Woolf

Whether you are reviewing your dream mentally in front of your dream altar or mapping the details on a large posterboard, you should remember to step back from the intricate pieces of your dream and ask yourself: *What is missing?* Sometimes the most telling piece of a dream is what isn't there. For example, if you dream about a wedding and have detailed imagery for getting dressed, the recessional, and the reception, then you are missing a central piece of the puzzle: the wedding vows and the partner. This kind of avoidance can sometimes give you clues about your innermost feelings and reactions to an idea. If Ricky includes "missing" information in his dream, he might discover that he is missing assistance (he gets out of a car and goes over the hole on his own) when overcoming his obstacle, and he doesn't need assistance to succeed.

The theme's the thing

Understanding the importance of a single dream can give you a snapshot of your world, but looking at several dreams over a span of time can give you a broader perspective. Using the mapping technique you can also bring together ideas and concepts from a series of dreams to find themes that run deeper and are stronger than the individual dream. Your dreams may have individual themes of confidence (Ricky's dream showed he needed only to make the decision to go ahead), patience, and the search for knowledge. Independently, these dreams can help you, but added together these ideas suggest that the changes in your life are not quick ones. A series of dreams (and the themes they communicate) can help you understand your divine messages without getting frustrated at the pace and the seemingly disparate topics of your dreams.

If you decide to map several dreams together, leave the central area open until most of the dream elements have been placed on the paper. The main focal point of your individual dreams will be on the B level of the map. Rather than exploring the symbolism of the dream elements, compare the elements of different dreams with each other. For example, perhaps both dreams involve water, but in one dream the water is flowing and bubbly, while in another dream the water is someone's sweat or a nearly dry creek bed. These comparisons and contrasts between elements are the goal of mapping dreams together.

Journal

Dream Pocket

To aid in understanding your dreams and gaining perspective, take some of your dream pillow along with your journal. Use a small envelope (or a folded business envelope) to seal a small amount of your dream herbs. Be sure to tape any loose seams, and then attach the envelope to the inside back cover of your journal. These will inspire you and help remind you of your dreamtime.

For your dream pocket try:

- A drop of ylang-ylang oil on a cotton ball (intuition).
- A drop of hazelnut oil (insight or wisdom).
- A small dried flower that contains many petal layers (layers of meaning).
- A small spider web, a dried leaf where the veins are visible, or cloth with a small print of flowers or geometric figures (for recognition of patterns).

Map your dream

Choose either a recent dream or one of the dreams you recorded in an earlier chapter and develop a map of the dream. If none of the focal points seem right for the A position, try using a summary of the dream's meaning for the main focal point or even leaving the center space blank. In dreams that have two or three fairly strong ideas, space these parts equally around the center of the page. While it is true that every dream has insight and possible information for you, not every dream has to be mapped for you to appreciate your connection to the Goddess's voice.

Layers of meaning

Identify a second dream and create a map. As you develop the map, focus on the body, mind, and spirit layers of understanding for each focal point and your associations. Expand your thinking about natural elements and spiritual aspects beyond the easy ideas. For the body, include the cycle of Nature, images of your body (in whole or only parts such as the hands), animals, etc. For the mind, include analytical thoughts, problem-solving, schools, classes, books, etc. Creativity can be included with either the body (the urge from Nature to create and procreate) or with the mind (creating art for the sake of beauty that is not exclusively functional). Choose three or four other layers and try to apply them to each dream element, but be sure to include the Spirit layer. As you continue to record your dreams, consciously choose different layers to apply to your dreams.

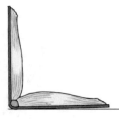

Personal patterns of interpretation

Just as the language of your dreams is unique to you, the best method for examining dreams is also personal. Develop a list of interpretation layers that works well for your dreams. You might also include a list of resources to help you understand your dreams (including the Internet and your Dream Pal). When you have trouble with a dream or its meanings, turn back to this list for ideas and suggestions that have worked for you in the past. Dream interpretation methods might include sketching, writing, talking, mapping, carving, collage, and recording your ideas.

Seven

Here and Now: Then and There

Once you have examined your personal symbols and themes, it is time to stand firmly on the dreamer's path and assess where you are and where you are going. This is where your path and the paths of other dreamers cross and perhaps merge. Every path for personal development reaches a point where you must gain perspective on yourself in relation to the world around you.

Dream Pal

Before you begin working on the next series of exercises, take a moment to list in your journal the gifts that you have found within your dreams. Have you achieved the goals you set earlier in this book for your dreaming? Why or why not? Do you believe that you will achieve them in the future? During your Dream Pal meeting, discuss your progress and celebrate the work you have done so far along the dreamer's path. What remaining goals or concepts do you have to explore in the world of dreams?

> *"The dream is the small hidden door in the deepest*
> *and most intimate sanctum of the soul, which opens*
> *into that primeval cosmic night that was soul long*
> *before there was a conscious ego and will be soul far*
> *beyond what a conscious ego could ever reach."*
>
> —C. G. Jung

Different types of dreams

Your dreams, while they are always personal, can be divided into categories that vary widely depending on the criteria. Dream interpreters and psychologists generally acknowledge dream categories that review the day's events (from the conscious mind), dreams with a greater significance (from the collective unconscious), and dreams in the realm of parapsychology. Dreams that fall under the parapsychology label include:

- Precognition: Knowledge of events before they happen (sometimes called clairvoyance).
- Astral travel: Travel of the soul on the astral plane of existence without the physical body
- Spiritual: A divine figure (Goddess, Christian Father-God, Jesus, etc.) appears within a dream, generally with a message; or a message is received regarding spiritual or moral activities.
- Telepathy: Sharing information between two people using only thoughts.
- Out-of-Body Experience (O.B.E.): Travel of your consciousness to other places and times in the regular waking world without your body (either in dreams or while awake).

Despite these interesting forms, it is important that you begin your dreaming experience by finding your connection with the Goddess and your sacred path. However, your sacred dreams will probably include, as a natural by-product, both precognitive dreams and spiritual dreams.

Daily and sacred dreams explored

Ancient Egyptians and dreamers on the island of Malta used the temples of their Goddesses and Gods to receive sacred dreams. Dreams were identified simply because the dreamer was in the temple, asked for a message from the Goddess, or because the dreamer was wealthy. Within the culture and life of antiquity, these rules for identifying sacred dreams from your run-of-the-mill dreams worked well, but both the world and dreaming have changed.

Daily dreams

During your early evening sleep, your mind performs a kind of mental housekeeping through daily dreams. The day's events are reviewed, your actions examined, and the vast amount of sensory information you receive is sorted. Important information is stored and trash information is thrown out. Dreams that process information from the day tend to be forgotten easily because they are common images, ideas, and emotions. The lower your emotional reaction, the less likely you are to remember the dream.

Just because these are common dreams does not mean that you should ignore them. Even these dreams can offer insight into your true feelings, thoughts, and desires. Working with the issues these dreams bring up will help you resolve them and clear the way for your sacred dreams. Sometimes your daily struggles (fear of failure, frustration, anger, desire, etc.) can become larger issues and overshadow the influence of the Goddess in your dreams.

Here are some fairly common "housekeeping" dreams:

- You relive the events of the day, but some portions are more intense than in reality.

- You dream of events from different aspects of your life (home, work, hobbies) mixed together.
- You might remember that you dreamed, but not that it was about a boat.
- You face obstacles and fears (your boss, a long list of errands, etc.) again and again without any significant change or insight.

Divine dreams

As the night progresses, however, your dreams will become less connected to the everyday world and more focused on Universal and Divine themes. Late at night is the most likely time for dreams of the Goddess, but divine dreams can happen at any time, really. Divine dreams tend to have a feeling of unexplained importance to them, which makes remembering them easier. Fear, hate, overwhelming love, loss, and surprise are just some of the strong human emotions that can give this dream its memorable power. Just because a dream is unpleasant doesn't mean it should be shoved into a corner and forgotten. Examining the dream could lead you to see a message of comfort or insight that was carried by the force of your emotions.

Dreamers from all walks of life, all spiritual paths, and all ages seem to agree on one thing: you simply "know" when a dream is from the Goddess. Her touch, to the dreamer, is unmistakable. This kind of knowledge cannot be taught or truly explained because it is an inner knowing that is born of faith. It is something that might be difficult to comprehend in a scientific world that demands reproducible experiments. This search for the provable dream experience can unfortunately leave you, the individual, with doubts and questions about your own power of observation. A flower that you see doesn't have to be shown to your family and friends to be beautiful. Take the dream experience, the flower of your night, and trust that it is beautiful for you. Understanding your spirit and trusting your inner voice, or gut instinct, is your best guide for identifying and exploring dreams of the Goddess.

Here are some examples of divine dreams:

- An item, scene, or person will be in hyperfocus, where that item appears to stand out from the surroundings and draw your attention.
- An item, scene, or person will be indistinct and difficult to focus on within the dream. The remainder of the dream is visually normal.
- Either during the dream or immediately upon waking you feel a sense of importance and mystery about the dream. Often, you might feel compelled to examine it.
- Important elements of the dream (such as the symbol on a book's cover) seem to need to be expressed, but these are often difficult pieces to explain using your current knowledge. The difficulty can arise because these images are not symbols and images already known to you. Often it is the case that you will shortly encounter the symbols used in the dream.
- Recurring dreams. These are issues and concepts that you are being shown for a reason; whether it is to improve your life or just to remove the problem so that your connection to the Goddess can grow deeper in your dreams.
- Events in the dream may follow the pattern of a Goddess myth. These myths may be mixed with imagery from your daily life. These mythical patterns often connect focal points in a dream.
- The Goddess in Her forms. The many goddesses from around the world may appear in your dreams in their historical, cultural, or recreated

images. For example, the Celtic Goddess Brigid
may have braids looped around her head and
knotwork on her dress.

- The Goddess in symbolic forms. Goddesses often
  have colors, items, forms, phrases, places, or animals that are associated with them. When these
  elements appear prominently in a dream it is
  likely that the Goddess associated with that item
  is adding her energy to the dream, hoping to
  draw your attention, or sending you a message.
  For example, the Santerian goddess Oshun rules
  the sea. Her symbols include shells, blue and white,
  sea creatures, and the moon that controls the tides.

- The Goddess may appear in an alternate form. A
  Goddess may choose to approach you in the
  dreamscape as a person you do not consciously
  recognize. The person may talk and act as if you
  are best friends. Often the Goddess will use this
  form for comfort and counseling when the recognition of Her would distract you from the message.

While it is true that all dreams are a balance of the Goddess, the Universe, and you, these three are not always equal
partners. As you resolve daily issues, you will open up to the
larger patterns of the Universe and the energy of the Goddess.
To dream entirely of the Goddess is as unbalanced as dreaming entirely of what you had for lunch. The strongest dreams
will probably happen when your dreaming life strikes a balance. Both new and experienced dreamers struggle with this
issue because daily dreams are familiar and easy while dreams of
the Goddess seem to be more elusive and mysterious.

Sarsen's dream: Star Woman Falls to Earth

One day Star Woman went walking in her garden in Galunlati,
the Great Above. She saw a plant growing there she had not seen

before and was curious, so she pulled it up. It made a great hole, the hole went right through the ground into the mystery below. Still curious, she looked into the hole. She fell through it and began to fall through the formlessness beneath....

Although this is just the beginning, Sarsen's dream recounts the tale of Star Woman and the creation of the world. Later in the dream, some of the details are significantly different from the original tale, but recounting traditional tales is a form of spiritual dream. The imagery within the dream is particular to Sarsen and the messages were definitely for her alone.

Understanding your faith

Recognizing dreams of the Goddess will be easier if you understand your perception of Her, your beliefs, and your sense of faith. Understanding the meaning and extent of the word *spirit* will help you identify dreams that connect to the *spiritual* side of yourself because her connection is a direct one to your spirit. For example, if you think of your spirit as residing near your heart and involving emotions and feelings, then you will, most likely, experience spiritual dreams as very emotional. However, if you view spirit as a combination of emotions, thoughts, and uniqueness, then your spiritual dream could involve an academic discussion as well as emotions. The exact meaning of *spirit* is less important than your comfort with the idea.

If your Spirit were a good friend, I would suggest taking a long Sunday afternoon to talk about the state of the world over coffee. Take time for understanding your thoughts, emotions, needs, worries, and beliefs surrounding your spirit and the Goddess. Your thoughts might fly quickly at first, but take each thought and compare it to the yardstick of your heart. This is the time to toss out the propaganda, as well as the "shoulds" and "cannots" that you might have learned while growing up. Breathe deeply three times, each one to calm the energy of your body, mind, and spirit. This will help you ground any negative energy and open your mind to the process.

Yardstick of the heart meditation

Ask yourself these questions:

- How do I visualize my spirit? (Does it have color, texture, or size?)

- Does my spirit contain emotion, thought, gut instinct, or some (or none) of these?

- What is my conception of the Goddess? Do I think that the Goddess exists within each part of creation, including me? Is the Goddess a part of, but separate from, creation, with her own form and independent thoughts, actions, and ideas? Is she something else entirely?

- How do I view the Goddess in relation to me? (Mother; sister; ancestor; great Creator; all powerful; powerful, but not controlling.)

- If my thoughts and beliefs about spirit have "always been," do I still feel the same way now, with the new experiences and understanding I have gained?

- I acknowledge that the world, my life, my teachers, and my chosen spiritual path all influence my thoughts and beliefs, and I can step aside from those beliefs. After examining my heart and mind independently, do I accept my previous beliefs and say that I still hold them to be true?

- Complete these sentences: "My spirit is...." "My spirit allows me to...." "I understand my spirit to be...."

- Looking at the elements of my own life, the parts that support my personal spirit are.... The parts that pull energy away from my spirit are....

- What is authentic to me in these beliefs and ideas? What ideas can I discard because they are true for society, my friends, etc., but not for me?

There are no correct answers for these questions, just knowledge about you. These answers may not always remain the same, so take time occasionally to return to these pages and these questions.

Then and there: prophetic dreams

*"When a society has no prophetic dreams,
there is no creativity."*

—Gregory Benford and
George Zebrowski

Probably the most celebrated (and argued) categories of dreams are those that appear to foretell future events. Some dream theorists have placed prophetic dreams clearly within the realm of belief, while others have explained the phenomena as a result of probability (dreaming of a car wreck in a transportation-dependent society) and the automatic process for the human mind to match patterns with known elements.

Unfortunately, for you as a dreamer, these dreams are mostly recognized after the event rather than before. Keeping a regular dream journal and working with your dreams on a consistent basis (even once a week) will increase your ability to recognize and examine prophetic dreams in advance. Recognizing dreams of the Goddess will also increase your connection to prophetic dreams because the two types of dreams are often subsets of each other. The present is your realm, the past is the realm of your ancestors and those of the human race, and the future is the domain of the Goddess. In order to understand the patterns of the future, you must first glimpse the past and present patterns along the web of the Universe, and then look, with the Goddess, forward into the future.

Prophetic dreams, if possible, are more elusive to identify than dreams of the Goddess. Most often they will include these characteristics:

- Exploration of future events (you are getting married, there is a car wreck, etc.).
- There is a warning quality to the message.
- You are told by the Goddess that the dream is a future event.
- The dream has a clear "reality" but isn't a situation you've experienced before.

Sarah's dream

I am together with my husband and two friends in a large theatre waiting on a performance. My husband and I walk outside and see Tom walking across the plaza away from the performance hall. I follow him (this is where I became lucid and watched the dream). I am with my husband and another group of other close friends and we are preparing for ritual. We go together to the showers that are in a dark, low-ceiling room, sand-bottomed, with large square tiles on the floor and walls. The water flows from above over ancient beams and we scrub with special stones and geodes. As we scrub the smell changes and we are cleaner. We move out to a sunlit patio where the large tiles can be seen and they have images of different gods and goddesses on them. I stand on one that is the guardian of children as we form a circle. I can look out into the bay, which is also tiled, and the water is very clear and distorted.

This dream falls into the category of both sacred and prophetic dreams. It is sacred because the dreamer felt it was important, the dream involves a sacred site (temple), and images of purification (shower) and the Goddess appear within the dream. All of these signs came together to get the dreamer's attention.

Sarah's dream also turned out to be prophetic. First, her life moved from the ordinary to a more spiritual focus (passive observance of a play to participating in a religous setting). Second, she left one group of friends for another. Third, Sarah found a connection to the Goddess that was pictured on the tile (her own Mother aspect). The dream gave her hints of upcoming transformations, probably to relieve any worries.

Wish fulfillment

Although Sarah's dream wasn't an example of wish fulfillment (she didn't want to leave her friends), prophetic dreams can be confused with wish fulfillment dreams. Wish fulfillment is the process of enacting through your dreams situations and experiences that you would like to have happen. For example, for single people who are seeking a mate or partner, dreaming often includes dates and marriage. You might dream of getting a raise for the efforts you put in at work last week, or of a spiritual initiation for the growth and progress you have made.

The line between wish fulfillment and prophetic dreams is impossible to draw because most people work toward making their dreams come true, and the future will be filled with the fruition from these plans. So, was it the dream that made the event happen, the work of the dreamer, fate, or some other combination of factors? If the outcome seems too good to be true, it may be wish fulfillment, but recognizing the influence of the Goddess within the dream may minimize some of the confusion. Few of the dreams from the Goddess will be purely wish fulfillment. The dreams will, more likely, contain some things that you desire and some unexpected outcomes as well. Perhaps you wanted a promotion and you dream of being unemployed at the beginning of a dream. Later on, in your dreamworld, you are searching for new work and the work you find isn't exactly what you expected (maybe another career), but it is a promotion of sorts. The combination of the desired result (promotion) with the confusing or distressing result (career change) could indicate the influence of the Goddess. Your dream is more than just wishing, it is a reassurance from the Goddess. The patterns and possibilities in a prophetic dream are generally just that: what is possible. The reality of the future is not a foregone conclusion. Even if an event happens just as your dream predicted, your actions before, during, and after the event are your own.

Ritual for sacred dreaming

Sacred and prophetic dreams can occur any time, but creating an environment that is supportive and openly receptive can bring these dreams more often. You probably don't have access to the dream temples of Rome, but creating sacred dream space within your life doesn't have to be an unbearable trial.

1. Reconnect with the Earth and find the calm center of your being, perhaps by using the body, mind, and spirit breathing technique. Begin preparing your sleeping space as a mini dream-temple in your bedroom. Acknowledge that you will be respectfully opening your dreams to the influence of the Goddess, perhaps with this chant:

   Dreams of power, Dreams of peace
   Goddess flower, My heart release.

2. Cleanse your room of any negativity that could linger from sharp words or the frustration of running late. Incense swirled in an ever larger spiral (moving counterclockwise) can be very effective at banishing negative energy from your sacred dream space. Whisper or say aloud:

   Within this space, let peace be.
   Gone are the doubts, gone are the needs.
   I clear this space for the Goddess and me.

3. Depending on your needs and your personal spiritual path, you may want to cast a circle that

includes you, your bed, and your bedroom. You can also simply reverse the direction of your incense saying:

> *I rest within this dreaming space*
> *to see the Goddess's face.*
> *She guides my dreams in peace*
> *My insights to increase.*

Alternately, you may wish to use a familiar chant or song that encourages you, strengthens your belief in your own inner knowledge, andconnects you with the Goddess.

4. Choose a dream pocket and add it to your dream pillow.

5. Light a candle that represents the influence of the Goddess in your sacred space. Just as the flame, your life dances around the central core of your being. The power to create and destroy is given to you within the dream world. Aloud, state the things that you intentionally destroy in order to create a sacred dream space: fear, doubt, tiredness, frustration, etc. These are the pieces that are burned within your candle flame tonight. Allow a moment or two for these ideas to dispel. (Alternately, you can write these words on small pieces of paper and place them in a censer to burn.)

6. Focus on the beams of light from the candle. These are the gifts and beauty of your dream world—small touches of the Goddess. Follow them as they touch your body and fall across your sleeping space. Concentrate on tracing as many of the beams as you can. The light of the Goddess surrounds you. Feel the beams move deeper and touch your soul. This is where Her light rests as you sleep. (Extinguish the candle.)

7. Either aloud or silently you should acknowledge the Goddess (in a specific aspect, if possible) and ask her to walk with you in the dreamscape. This request can take the form of a prayer, a song, a visualization of walking together, or a simple statement such as, "Great Mother, Goddess, and Sister, tonight I open my heart and mind to you in my dreams. Please let me feel your presence." (Be careful here. Asking "to see what you need to know" can sometimes give you information you don't want.)

8. In your favorite position, sleep with the Goddess as your companion. As you close your eyes and prepare to relax, remember Her touch from the candle and the safe space you created to cherish this connection.

9. Once you have recorded your dream in the morning, release the circle of protection and thank any guardians who watched your sacred dream space.

Inspiring the prophetic dream

When you are prepared for a night of sacred sleep and can reasonably expect to awaken with enough time to record your dreams, divinatory or prophetic dreaming can be encouraged. Here are some suggestions:

- Place an item on your dream altar that relates to the person, place, or idea about which you wish to dream: your mother's pendant, a spouse's key chain, or a picture of the possible event (wedding picture for wedding).

- Write your question on a small piece of paper and attach it to your dream pillow with a safety pin. You can also tie it in a scroll and leave it on your altar.

- Learn from the methods of the ancients and follow a pattern of purification and concentration for sacred sleep that includes ritual bath for cleansing, light meals (without meat if possible), clean and orderly sleeping chamber, and undisturbed sleep.

- Involve your senses with aromatherapy, music, water fountains, etc.

- To dream about events related directly to you in the near future, review the past few entries in your dream journal. Do not despair if these entries are not consecutive, few people manage daily dream entries. Trace the energy, themes, and problems within your dreams over the recent past. Reading the entries will give you a sense of your life's pattern, even if your understanding is subconscious.

- To dream about events not directly related to you, find a way to connect with the energy of that person, place, or situation. Talk to that person (even on unrelated topics), visit a specific location, view pictures of it, or perhaps make an idea map of a specific situation including people, concerns, questions, and goals for the dream.

Prophecy and the present

The most difficult problem with prophetic dreams is discovering what the information means to you and your world. Dreamers frequently complain that prophetic dreams are the most disturbing because the information is unwelcome, uncomfortable, or distressing. In Sarah's case, knowing that her life was changing could have caused her distress. Raindance didn't identify the dream as prophetic until after the events, but the subconscious message helped anyway.

Prophetic dreams can seem negative, but your perspective of them and what you choose to do with them can make a big difference. Pat, a cancer patient, diagnosed her own breast cancer through a dream (definitely a body-layer) and caught it before it was too far gone to treat. Although she struggled with it, her dream gave her enough warning to have a fighting chance. Pat's use of dreams to treat her illness continues the traditions started by Hippocrates (from approximately 450 B.C.E.), an early doctor who would frequently use the symbols and "recipes" revealed in his dreams to diagnose and treat patients. Perhaps the most influential dream interpreter, however, was a man named Artemidorus (approximately 140 B.C.E.) who wrote *Oneirocritica* (*The Interpretation of Dreams*), a book that separated the superstition of dreaming from proven methods for interpretation. These instructions for dream interpreters by Artemidorus took into account, for the first time, the personality of the dreamer.

A dreamer's personality and emotions can help reveal powerful dreams as well as prophetic ones. Death, loss, children, marriage, and fears are common subjects for this kind of dream. Establishing a pattern of prophetic and divinatory dreams can be exciting and powerful, but a wise woman once told me, "Be careful what you wish for, you may get it." Choosing to dream in the prophetic realms may connect you with more of the Goddess's power, but the responsibilities that come with that kind of power are sometimes overwhelming.

Once you have conceived a prophetic dream, you have a few choices to make. Do you share the information? Do you act to change the events? Do you forget the dream and let events happen naturally? Sometimes you may feel like the information is too important to restrict to your journal, but sharing the information can cause a world of trouble and upset for yourself as well as other people.

Imagine that you dream about a friend's unexpected death. Sharing the dream with your friend can have a number of results; some positive, some scary, and some completely un-expected. It is your choice to share and your friend's decision whether or not to act on the information. In every situation, make the decision that measures best against your spirit. If you want to tell your friend, but your heart has doubts, then follow your heart's instincts. Your spirit will guide you to the best path if you listen honestly.

In many ways, the prophetic dream is like any kind of divinatory process, the meanings and influence rely on your interpretation. The symbols and information have been pre-sented because the Goddess and the patterns of the Universe responded to a question from you (spoken or not). You should accept the information from the dream as an answer meant for you from the Goddess.

Journal

Dream Pocket

Knowing the future includes knowing your own strength. Choose a fabric with a strong color and a small pattern to symbolize the patterns of the Universe that are present in prophetic dreams.

For your dream pocket try:

- ◆ Laurel tree or bay leaves (divination and premonitions).
- ◆ Vanilla (comfort of home to avoid bad dreams).
- ◆ Geranium leaves, especially from the aromatic cousin the lemon or mint geranium plants (grounding).
- ◆ Patchouli incense or a dollar bill (wealth).
- ◆ Comfry (health).

Choose your dream and encourage it

Create sacred dream space for three nights and record the results of your sacred sleep. Did your altar objects or the Goddess appear? Did you sleep soundly and wake without recalling anything? Did you dream and have vivid details? Describe any sensations that might have been different from your regular sleep patterns. Think about your emotional reactions and initial thoughts related to the dream. Do you believe that this is a sacred dream, a dream of prophecy, a dream of mental housekeeping, or something else? Did you awake with a sense of lightness, excitement, importance, etc.?

If you choose to make a dream map of your experiences, remember to add whether an object or idea was related to your altar or your question.

Dreams of the Goddess

Using the mapping techniques from Chapter 6, map any dreams that result from the previous journal prompt. Be sure to include a note about the influence of the Goddess that you felt. If none of your dreams were spiritual you may wish to wait a few days and try the previous journal prompt again. Did one object seem to draw your attention? Did the people behave oddly? Do you feel that any of the details in the dream were put there intentionally by the Goddess? What associations or meanings could these objects have for you spiritually?

Discussing with your Dream Pal

Plan to enjoy sacred sleep on the same night as your Dream Pal. If possible, choose four nights where you can alternate sacred sleep and regular sleep. In your meeting with your Dream Pal, discuss the differences between these nights. You might also compare notes on what you dreamed and see if there are similarities between you, especially on sacred sleep nights.

Prophetic dreams

If you choose to explore the world of prophetic dreams, record the time and place when the dream occurred and the time and place when you think the events of the dream will occur. In your dream journal, you might include suggestions about what the dream could be referring to. Sometimes it is helpful to review your old dream journals for prophetic dreams. If you had dreams that came true, what emotions surrounded these dreams? Were the people familiar? Is there a pattern to these dreams? This information could help you understand your own pattern of naturally occurring prophetic dreams and make them easier to recognize in the future. If you have not had proiphetic dreams, what would you like to know about the future? What are your obstacles to this kind of dreaming?

Eight
Lucid Dreaming:
Acting in Your Own Dreams

To date, you have probably sailed along somewhat smoothly by examining your dreams in the waking world, but your understanding can reach greater depths when you combine the awareness of being awake with your divine dreams. The depths of lucid dreaming are alluring for the novelty, the richness of spirit, and the stories they create to tell your friends; but these depths come at a price. In reaching beyond your current limitations, you reach both forward to the future and behind you to the beginnings of mankind. The journey you undertake in seeking out the Goddess in your dreams is as much an inner journey to recognition as it is an outer journey to understanding. The Goddess runs throughout the world and within you.

Lucid dreams

Lucid dreams are generally defined as dreams where you recognize that your experiences are within a dream and are separate from your waking reality—all while you are still asleep. Some definitions of lucid dreaming require that the dreamer

be awake and able to act within the dream. Lucid dreams can give you the uncomfortable feeling of disconnection from yourself because you are in two places at once: within the dream and asleep in bed. This unnerving dual perspective can defeat your goal of lucid dreaming by waking you up.

Working with dreams in the waking world is fairly objective, but working within the world of dreams is completely subjective. The truth of your experiences is completely up to you. You will have to rely on yourself to recognize the dream.

The fine print on lucid dreaming

"Almost everyone wants interpretations instead of the dream.
I want the dreams to continue to well up out of them, which
means to a great degree in their own terms. So the powerful
ones remain insofar as possible objects of contemplation more
than of analysis. A dream is a glimpse of a dimension,
and translating it is like saying of a poem,
'In other words, you mean....'"

—W. S. Mervin

Before undertaking a journey into sacred dream space and the world of lucid dreaming, you should probably check your baggage. Many of the ideas and assumptions that are made about lucid dreams should firmly be left at home on this trip because you will not be able to reach sacred space or lucidity with them. Some common ideas you should leave behind:

*The idea that you **must** achieve a state of lucid dreaming.*

Just because there is another path to take doesn't mean it is the right one for you. Look at your own needs, wants, and desires for dreaming. Use the techniques and suggestions you find in this book if they are useful for you. Skip the pieces that don't resonate with your heart. Some people are naturally aware during their dreams, for others, it takes a great deal of practice, and still others never attain lucid dreaming. Each of the ideas suggested in this chapter for lucid dreaming could be adapted for inducing dreams. Your spiritual path can develop, grow, and blossom with the use of any (or none) of the dream techniques and ideas presented up to this point.

In order for it to be lucid, you must change the dream or act on conscious decisions.

Dreamers who consciously observe their dreams are just as aware (or lucid) as dreamers who make changes. The observing dreamer does make one change to the dream, he changes his own perspective. Even though the ability to act is sometimes heralded as the greatest gift of lucid dreaming, each act is a choice made in a world that is delicately balanced between you, the Goddess, and the Universe. Maintaining that balance is tricky in lucid dreams.

The idea that more is better.

Your mind needs a rest from both the biological and psychological effects of lucid dreaming. Your mind is already in a heightened state of awareness during dreaming and just before a lucid dream you receive an extra burst of energy along the neural pathways. Trying to achieve constant lucid dreaming would deprive your mind of time to recover and rejuvenate from the day, not to mention overloading your mind's circuitry. Be selective in the time and placement of changes in your dreams. Too much control over your dreams may drown out the message you are working so hard to hear!

The idea that you've handled all of your emotional issues and are free and clear.

If one thing has stood out in years of dreaming, it is the power dreams have to point out personal flaws in infinite detail. If you have doubts, hesitations, or concerns about lucid dreaming, dream meanings, or your own power as a dreamer, then you will find these obstacles holding you back when you try to "wake up" in dreams. Working with those ideas, instead of ignoring them, is the only way to get past this hurdle.

Now that you know which assumptions will be trouble-some for you in lucid dreaming, here are some ideas that will be helpful in your journey:

Set a purpose for your dream, not a goal.

Specific questions can unnecessarily focus a dream on one aspect of life when the truest message of the Goddess is a broader topic. The best way to avoid this problem is to establish a purpose for dreaming. A purpose provides the reason for pursuing and continuing the dream process as opposed to a goal that sets a specific end result. Once you reach a goal, you must find another goal to continue your dreaming work. With a purpose, you can continue to dream for years seeking "a deeper connection" or "understanding the influence of the Goddess."

The idea that if you've got to ask a question, make it good.

Asking the Goddess to give you insight into your daily life is most likely not going to reveal anything you don't already know. Look into your own heart and honestly look for the answer first. A teacher once said to me, "Don't ask questions you don't want the answer to." At the same time a billboard proclaimed that, "The only stupid question is the one un-asked." You might begin your dreaming with the Goddess believing the second statement, but in the end, the first statement holds more strength for you. Most sacred dreamers start out wanting to ask questions that are deeply based in spirit ("Why am I here?" "What is my path?" etc.). These questions are difficult to answer clearly, even with perfect communication. Until you understand some of the nuances of your connection to the Goddess, take time to ask smaller questions and then progress toward the spiritual questions. Or, simply allow the spirit information to flow into your dreams naturally.

Lucid dreams can help with everyday life, including children's dreams.

The benefit of this mental awareness is that you can consciously choose to remember the dream in greater detail, look closely at your surroundings, and make changes within the dream. Lucid dreams can be used to practice speeches (changing the delivery so that you are satisfied), visualize upcoming challenges (such as asking for a raise), or exploring the possibilities for a situation. Even children's television programming uses the concepts of lucid dreaming to teach children to change frightening dreams into something more child-friendly.

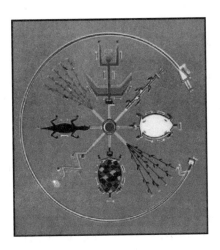

Inducing lucid dreams

"We are all artists in our dreams."

—Fredrich Nietzsche

Many of the techniques described for inducing prophetic dreams (Chapter 7) will also work for lucid dreaming. Just as a smile helps you feel better, your dreams will mirror what you do. From the following list, try to select a technique that matches your need for the dream (puzzles for solving a problem, imagery for creativity, etc.). Review these techniques and remember to create sacred space before you begin these exercises.

- Before going to bed, do intensive puzzles that tax your mind or play complex computer games. Scientific investigation has shown that lucid dreams are often preceded by a short burst of activity in the mind of the dreamer, similar to the brainwave activity of someone who is problem-solving.

- Listen to classical or instrumental music. You might have heard that playing this music helps develop complex neural patterns within children's brains, but it also helps to reinforce the patterns that are present within *your* brain. This is a technique that you can use while showering, while doing the evening dishes, or instead of the last half-hour of junk television you might watch before going to bed.

- When you are inducing dreams with the idea of connecting with the Goddess, remember to invite images and places that have a sense of comfort for you. If the Goddess has previously come to you in dreams at a lake, a house, or a mountain path, then work with that imagery. The imagery will have meaning for you because it has been used before in your connection with the Goddess. If you feel that the Goddess has not been present in your dreams, try using the places and times you listed as spiritual (page 104).

- Study and meditate on mandalas and labyrinths to encourage pattern recognition and meditative states of mind.

- Place a pair of eyeglasses on your altar to cue your mind to "see" within the dream.

- Choose your diet carefully. Foods such as salmon (fatty compounds) and vegetables (B vitamins) contain nutrients beneficial for dreaming.
- Take a multi-vitamin rich in B-6 and B complex vitamins.

Recognizing the lucid dream

In order to explore the world of lucid dreaming, you need to know that you are dreaming while it happens. The following are some ways that you can recognize your dreams:

- Shocking events: While it is within the normal realm of life for someone to be in a car wreck, it would be very odd if the wreck involved your child coming home from school on the local space shuttle. Ask yourself if the events are possible, but remember that even real life can be improbable at times.
- Observer: You have the feeling of being an observer rather than a participant in the events around you. Try looking at your hands or your reflection in the mirror. When you are awake, your hands should appear solid and should feel normal when you touch them. Dreamers have described looking at their hands as if they are at a great distance.
- Clarity: The colors and sensations of dreams are described as being very striking. Your lucid dream might appear to be in very sharp focus or to have almost cartoon-bright colors.
- Cue images: You can train your mind to insert a certain object or image within a dream to let your dreaming self know that you are dreaming. This is easiest with an object that is not part of your daily life (antique key, statue, etc.).

- Inner knowledge: You may explain your lucid dreams with the classic statement, "I just know." The more you know about your own dream world, the more likely you are to recognize it as a dream while you are there.

If you are uncertain about whether you are dreaming or awake, try testing your world to see if the rules of reality or the rules of dream apply. Here are some of the tests of the physical world commonly used among lucid dreamers:

- Clap your hands. Clapping may make a sound, but not feel like clapping on your hands (or vice versa).
- Imagine effortlessly flying off the ground or passing your hand through a solid object (slowly).
- Try communicating a conversation or thought to someone solely using telepathy.
- These small tests are easier if you keep them within the context of the original dream. For example, if you are in an early American saloon in the wild wild West, try ordering a cappuccino which works with the idea of a bar but is different enough to confirm that you are dreaming). If you get the drink, you're probably dreaming.
- Read something once, look away, and read it again. If the words remain the same, you're probably not dreaming.

Successful lucid dreamers begin using these testing techniques in everyday reality so that it becomes a habit to test the world around you in subtle ways. Eventually, you will take this reality-checking habit into the dreamscape and be able to recognize when you are dreaming.

Remaining in the dream

Many first-time lucid dreamers report recognizing the dream world and then waking up immediately. Your mind is unprepared for the strange images and ideas of the lucid dream, and will wake you in self-defense. Immediately returning to sleep will probably put you back in the same dream. If you are too awake to go back to sleep, recording the dream may give you a piece of information that you can use for future meditation and dream induction. It is important that you either return to sleep immediately or attempt to record the dream if you are awakened suddenly. This will prevent the dream images from bothering you as incomplete thoughts.

Once you have learned to relax and let the shock of realizing you are dreaming fade, you should be able to remain as an observer in your dreams. Strong emotions, whether they are good or bad, can shock you out of your dreams and into wakefulness. Although it may sound contradictory to seek a personal connection with the Goddess and remain emotionally detached, that is exactly what is needed for effective lucid dreaming. Allow yourself to have emotions, but note them in the background as part of your dreaming experience and not part of your awareness at the moment. If you become involved in the emotional energy of the dream, you are likely to ignore the symbolic and spoken messages of the Goddess. Lucid dreaming as a sacred act requires that you step slightly aside from yourself and recognize your place as one of three energies intertwined in the dream world. In order to see the dream's entire meaning you must gain a perspective that is not limited to your own.

Here are some additional hints for remaining within a lucid dream:

- If you recognize you are within a dream and the scenery begins to fade, increase sensory input for your senses within the dream (touch is generally the last to fade in a dream). The sensations will force your dreaming self to focus on the dream and not on the returning reality.

♦ If you are within a dream and feel as if your awareness is slipping or you are waking up, try the "spinning" technique. Make your dreaming body spin like a top while repeating the affirmation that "the next thing I see will be in a dream."

♦ Accepting the differences between the waking world and the dream world will help you to remain in the dream world rather than being jolted into waking reality. Knowing that your dreams, your experiences, and the insights of the dream cannot harm you, and that they are specifically there to help you, can help you remember to stay calm during stressful dreams.

♦ If you wake from a dream and remember it clearly, close your eyes and imagine you are back within the dream. What is the next thing that happens? What do you hear next?

During Sarah's dream she is able to reach a state of lucid dreaming. After becoming lucid outside the theatre, she is able to explore the dream experience with her senses and remember an amazing amount of detail (the original dream was much longer). Although she does not actively try to manipulate the dream world, each time she looks closer at something, she opens up to receiving more information. For example, without conscious choice she might never have looked down at the tiles on the patio where the guardian of children was pictured. This detail became available to Sarah because she was lucid and she can choose to explore the Goddess Kwan Yin and any insights that she might offer.

Ritual dream space

"The poem is altar for the dream."

—David Ray

The obvious path is not always the best one, and the sleeping path is not always the way to begin lucid dreaming. Preparation before you sleep is as important or more so than the work you will do while you are dreaming. Prepare a space for lucid dreaming by following your usual nightly pattern. You should pay special attention to:

- Your dream altar (to focus the reason you are seeking a lucid dream).

- Removing distractions (including before, during, and after sleep). Distractions also include negative attitudes or issues of self-respect, personal identity, responsibilities, or control issues.

- Creating sacred space within the physical waking world (this will set the pattern for the sacred dream space and help the energy of the dream connect with your own awareness).

- Using chants or rhythmic motion as a form of meditation. These are ancient techniques that will be useful within the sacred space to focus your energy on dreaming. The same brain waves that are present in deep meditation are present during lucid dreams.

- Making room for sacred dreaming in your morning. This will allow you to record and review your waking dreams within sacred space. More insights might be available to you in the safety of your own ritual space.

As is the case with all sacred space, entering the dream world with an open, receptive, and positive attitude is an essential tool for lucid dreaming. The bedtime rituals and preparations you have practiced up to this point will help reinforce the idea that dreaming is a consecrated act. Being sure of your purpose for dreaming will also help to alleviate doubts that could disrupt you during the dream.

Creating sacred dream space

The creation of sacred space within the dream world should be handled with the same care and attention that you would give to any waking ritual. Sacred space should always have a feeling of safety, comfort, power, and personal peace for you. As you reach lucidity, you can choose to mirror the ritual you performed before you slept, or you can create a new circle. Many of the European and indigenous religious traditions create sacred space by cleansing the area and calling for both safety and blessings. Typically they form a circle that is symbolic of the cycle of life. Regardless of the type of circle you create, be sure that it does not disrupt the dream imagery that exists when you become lucid. For example, if you are outdoors, you might include natural elements in your circle.

For many Pagan and Neo-Pagan spiritual paths, the four directions and their corresponding natural Elements—North (Earth), East (Air), South (Fire), and West (Water)—are used as protection in sacred space. Some native traditions call on the spirits of the ancestors for guidance and protection. For your sacred space, you may choose to ask for protection and help from the Elements, the ancestors, or nothing at all.

If you choose not to dream lucidly, or it has not yet become easy for you, meditate on the idea of creating sacred space within the dream world. Imagine your motions as you sweep away the negative energy and hear your voice as you invite protection and blessings from the dream world. As you lie down to dream, focus on a place that gives you a particularly strong connection to the Goddess or the sacred in your life.

By thinking about this place before you sleep, you are more likely to encounter it in your dreamscape and more likely to meet the Goddess within your dreams.

Journal

Dream pocket

Lucid dreaming brings with it many possibilities and many doubts. Use a white cloth for this dream pocket (or silver for the moon) to invoke protection and guidance.

For your dream pocket try:

- Moonflowers (lucid dreaming).
- Morning glory seeds (lucid dreaming, awaking refreshed).
- Clear sage (protection).
- Sandalwood (spirituality).

Recognize again the sacredness of dream space

Create a brief outline of the nightly ritual you perform before going to bed. What changes have you made to encourage dreaming? What special actions do you take to create sacred space for dreaming? This description of your sacred dreaming ritual will benefit you when you are busy and stressed and cannot remember the things that worked. If you are still working to find your own ritual pattern, list the elements you have tried and the results.

Lucid dreams

Record your dreams for a period of two weeks. During the two weeks, practice the techniques for testing your reality. In addition to recording your dreams and working with the layers of meaning for each symbol, make note of any dreams where you become lucid. At what point do you realize you are dreaming? Do you just "wake up" or is there a clue that tipped you off?

Make sure to note whether you were an observer or an active participant in the dream and whether you made any changes. What changes did you make? What changes would have been possible within the context of your dream? Consider the possible outcome of the dream without your changes. You might wish to write this alternate form of the dream within your journal.

Sacred dream space

Whether you are able to achieve lucid dreaming or work with inducing dreams, you are still forming sacred space within the dream. How well do your dreams reflect the imagery and energy of your waking sacred space? Make note of any similarities and differences between the waking and dreaming space and why these might exist. Does your dream space have a natural or man-made construction? Were you successful at creating this space and calling on a familiar Goddess? Why or why not? You might alter the way you create sacred space and note any changes in your dreaming space.

Nine
Dreams With a Purpose

"Dreams are the wanderings of the spirit through all nine heavens and all nine earths."

—Lu Yen

Step by step you have walked the dreamer's sacred path toward the Goddess. Each step along the way has given you a tool, a bit of knowledge, or an insight to your personal dreaming. Through the lucid dreaming techniques in the previous chapter you learned to become aware and conscious during both waking and dreaming reality. Your awareness is essential for opening your mind fully to both the experience and the message of your dreams. And now you have come full circle to the altered dream states that the ancients used to understand their dreams. With intention and focus, your dreams can become a sacred place of learning and growth—a place to meet the Goddess.

Sacred space has been defined in many ways, but mostly it is space that is entered with reverence and openness, which can create a sense of deep spiritual connection, comfort, and separateness. The sacred sites of the world feel different to visitors who are aware of energy in cathedrals, labyrinths, sweat

lodges, and mountains. In order for you to connect to the sacred energy and the Divine, you need to remain aware of your intentions, of your sacred purpose for dreaming.

Reflections on dreams and reality

The thoughts you have just before sleep are most likely to be the ones that influence your dreams. Choose these thoughts carefully and focus on your sacred dreaming space. In reality, your circle creates an outer sanctuary in the waking world and then you carry the energy of that sanctuary into an inner and more personal sanctuary of the dream world—a temple within a temple. Your bedtime rituals that cleanse, bless, and prepare your sleeping place can cleanse and prepare the dreaming space as well. Entering the inner sanctuary of dreams becomes easier when you feel protected in the outer world. As you fall asleep and pass into the dream sanctuary, you also take with you a firm sense of your identity as an individual. You are still you, and that knowledge should comfort you.

You cannot, however, take with you into dreams the filters and defenses that separate you from the world around you. Each of these filters, although it protects you from the negative energy that can influence you on a daily basis, serves as a barrier to your connection with the Goddess. In order to dream with the Goddess you must lose these filters and defenses. Just before you pull up the covers, or even as you lie in bed, remove these filters like layers of excess clothing. Take a breath for body, mind, and spirit, and release your worries, concerns, and anxieties about each of these parts of your life. With these cleansing breaths, release any of your filters that are cynical about good news, any internal editors that denounce your thoughts, and the social commentator who says you "should" do something. If one part of your life (job, children, romance, etc.) is giving you particular problems, then release these concerns in a separate breath.

Once you have descended (either lucidly or through dream induction) into sacred dream space, you may do the things that dreamers do; that is, anything you want. Ask questions, look around, seek your own personal path, or inquire about the future. Once you have formalized your intentions within the dream world as sacred, you can do any work that needs to be done. Rituals and magickal workings can have any purpose—the options are an endless reflection of you and your needs. In ritual dream space, you could ask for strength, get help releasing fear, do a spell to reveal your next career move, and so on.

During waking rituals, people within sacred spaces often raise energy for a purpose through chanting, movement, prayer, or sympathetic actions (such as tying two strings to indicate two hearts united). If these actions suit your purpose, then go for it! Keep in mind, however, that changing your dream too much (you were outside in your dream and you make the dream move inside or involve many new characters) can really affect your dream space. A subtle shift in the pieces of a dream (such as adding your ritual tools or a partner) will make it more likely that the energy will be maintained without disturbing your connection to the Goddess.

Because long dreaming sessions last about 30 minutes, and lucid dreaming time is approximately equal to real time, you should know that time is of the essence. Varying sleep and dream cycles make it difficult to guess how long your brain can sustain a lucid dream, so don't dally! Understanding your purpose before you pass from outer ritual space to the inner dream space will save you worry, energy, and time.

Once you have finished your ritual within the dream and your time in the sacred dream space begins to come to a close, you should thank the Goddess for Her insights and close the inner sanctuary of your dreams. What you thank Her for is completely up to you, but dreamers often report that truly sacred dreams of the Goddess imbue them with a sense of power, strength, insight, love, and connection with the Goddess.

Dreamers also feel as if their independent identity has been transformed into an understanding of themselves as an intricate piece of the whole of Life. The items you had as you dipped your hand into the dream well of the Goddess (doubt, fear, questions, etc.) can be changed and inspired. By cupping your hand in anticipation you can draw a bit of water containing insight and energy toward the surface. A bit of the energy that comes from the Goddess will resurface with you to the waking world.

Personal sacred space in dreams

In your journal, develop the idea of your ideal personal sacred space. Use your knowledge of symbolism and your connection to the Goddess to create a space that is warm, welcoming, and inviting for you. Maybe your sacred space is hidden in a cloud, a treetop, a cave, a river, or an ancient site of power such as the pyramids in Egypt or the standing stone circles in Ireland. Include (through description, drawings, or clippings) the edges of your space, the colors, the places where you sit and meditate, and the places where the Goddess enters these sacred spaces. You are in control and the rules of the waking world don't apply.

Once you have described this space, choose an object or an image if you have created one (the beach, a seashell, or a pinecone for natural forest) that can succinctly represent your sacred space. Place your representation of sacred dream space on your dream altar and study the details with your eyes open. Close your eyes and try to recreate the image of the object exactly as it appears. Now look at the object (mentally) from above and below. Creating realistic images within your mind will help develop a personal connection to the space and increase your ability to travel there in your dreams. Now use your mind to look at the personal sacred space you have created. Study the details, how the light falls onto the ground, the sounds, and colors. Become familiar with your space from every angle. You might store your description of sacred dream-ing space (written or drawn) on paper tied into a scroll. Stand the scroll on your dream altar when you wish to attract that space. This is especially helpful if you have difficulty with lucid dreams but still wish to focus on sacred dreams.

Sarah's sacred space

Although Sarah did not normally choose a stone temple as her sacred space (from Chapter 7), the idea was easier to work with once she had been there in the dream world. She did not need to create a separate sacred space immediately after she became lucid because her dreams had handed her one already made. In her journal, Sarah developed sketches and descrip-tions of the two places at the temple she had already explored: the cleansing shower room and the outdoor ritual patio. In her journal she also noted places in these rooms that she would have liked to look. On the patio, there were standing stones that seemed important, but Sarah did not have time to ex-plore the first time. When she creates personal sacred space she may choose to incorporate some of the elements from her dream (running water, geodes, etc.). Doing this could help her induce a dream of the sacred temple and allow her to ex-plore the other areas, including her connection to the Goddess. Sarah can also use this sacred space as an easy point of refer-ence to explore her relationship with the guardian of children. Because this Goddess has already appeared in symbolic form, asking this goddess to appear (through meditation, invoca-tion, or by placing a drawn image of the tile on a dream altar) could deepen Sarah's relationship with the Goddess and her own spirituality.

Divine invitation

Once you have created sacred space, whether it is within your bedroom or your dream, you can invite the presence of the Goddess. For many dreamers the presence of the Goddess is evident in the themes and insights of their dreams, and that is enough. Other dreamers need a familiar figure in order to relate to the Goddess. If you choose to call the Goddess to appear, begin by invoking a goddess you are familiar with. If you already have a statue of Quan Yin or Brigid, then use these faces on your altar and within your sacred dream. Understanding the ideas, likes, and dislikes of a particular goddess strengthens your connection to her and increases the strength of your invocation.

Invocation of the Goddess Inanna:

I beckon to thee, gentle morning star,

Inanna, keeper of the heavenly swirls,

Bring to me insight and the Unity you are,

And walk with me between the worlds.

Invocations such as this are easier to remember if they rhyme and have been practiced. Although it may feel like a painful English class, writing invocations can help you clarify both your intent and your image of the Goddess. Notice that Inanna is associated in this invocation with the heavens, the morning star, perspective, and unity. These are the aspects that will be most strongly apparent in a dream where she has been called. Inanna could also be called on for divination, matters of law, leadership, and even wine making! Your invocations can be as short or as detailed as you wish, but they should have meaning for you personally and for the specific need in your sacred dream.

Whether you created sacred space and invoked the Goddess in your dreams or not, you may still want to acknowledge the presence of the Goddess at the end of your dream with a prayer. Invocations and prayers are the most basic form of sacred connection: the one that recognizes a special bond between the human spirit and the Divine. For example:

Mother of Wisdom and light,

I find you, Sophia, within the weave of my dreams.

Thank you for guiding me here, for lending me your insight

And your patience within this sacred realm.

Dreaming with the Goddess begins by consciously recognizing Her presence within the dream and the importance that Her influence holds for you. It is your inner acknowledgement of the Goddess's influence that changes the dream world from something the Goddess gives you into something you share with Her. When you begin to share the dream world with the Goddess, you begin a give and take relationship that can be very powerful.

Once you have invited the Goddess to join you within your sacred dreamscape, wait. This is probably the hardest part of sacred dreams—waiting with an open mind. This waiting is similar to the point in meditation where you allow your mind to forget the daily concerns and questions, and you relax into simply being. Spend a moment just existing within the dream.

As you near the end of your dream, or you begin to feel yourself waking, remember to acknowledge the insights of the Goddess. Release the circle and sacred space within your dream (even if it is just with a motion of your hand) before you leave your sacred dream space. You will need to release these same energies in the waking world as well. Remember that these two worlds mirror and reflect each other. Leaving the Element of Fire unattended can cause quite a stir in your dreams and in your bedroom!

Meeting the strange Goddess

Some of the best dream advice I ever received was from my mother. "Try a little bit of everything, you never know when your tastes will change." Although she was talking about vegetables at the time, the advice holds true for spiritual journeys as well. The familiar is a safe haven for you, a place where you can relax your guard because the pieces are all known. Exploring with a familiar Goddess is comfortable and can build your confidence in sacred dreams. There is nothing to threaten you, and most probably there is nothing to challenge you, either. The strongest insights and connections are sometimes made after your original ideas have been confronted with a different viewpoint. The new perspective of the many faces of the Goddess can give you insight into yourself.

Take time in your dreaming to explore and dream with the many faces of the Goddess. Each Goddess has Her strengths, insights, and Her own perspective on your path in the world. As you walk your path, you may want to call on the strength and creativity of Kali, but without understanding Her beforehand, you may hesitate (Kali is a Goddess of chaotic change as well as powerful creation). Dreams can offer you a place to meet Kali, take tours of Her temples, review Her history and learn to understand the particularly powerful energy that She carries. Ask to learn Her stories, Her expectations, and Her place along your path. She may not be the Goddess that belongs with you on your path, but understanding Her energy will help you gain a deeper respect of the Divine power that is part of the Mother Goddess.

Getting to know all about Her

Before dreaming with an unfamiliar Goddess you should do a little research. Go deeper than Her name and place of origin. Imagine that this is a person you have just met. What questions do you ask when you want to get to know someone better? "Where are you from?" "What brings you here?" "What do you do?" These are typical questions you might ask a would-be friend. For the Goddess, the questions are very similar. Here is a sample list of questions that can help you learn and grow to understand the Goddess (or even a friend or a spirit guide in the dream world). Individually or combined, these make excellent meditation questions for your sacred dreaming. You might use these as the purpose for your dream with a particular Goddess:

1. What is She the Goddess of (animals, oceans, mountains, love, etc.)?

2. What is sacred to Her (an animal, place, food, time of year, etc.)?

3. What are Her attributes? Describe only the strongest aspects of Her as if someone wanted an introduction to your Goddess.

4. Complete this sentence: "My Goddess is the one who... (carries me through childbirth, encourages wealth, etc.)."

5. Describe an image of your Goddess as a piece of art (statue, picture, amulet, living artwork, etc.). What symbols are incorporated in the representation? Why?

6. Who worships Her? How?

7. How is a true follower of your Goddess recognized? What kind of person does She protect or take an interest in?

8. How does this Goddess to intercede on your behalf? In what situations would She act or not act?

9. What places, events, actions, seasons, or Elements are associated with your Goddess?

10. Why would someone have an altar to Her? Where is the altar? What is on it?

11. What are appropriate offerings for Her?
12. Are there any rites of passage or experiences that your Goddess presents as challenges to Her followers regularly?
13. What kind of ritual is appropriate for this Goddess?
14. Write an invocation to your Goddess.
15. What are Her negative aspects? What happens if She is displeased?
16. Where does your Goddess touch you (belong on your path)?

In the Appendix there are a few brief descriptions of goddesses and their origins. Use these goddesses as a beginning point for your sacred dreams, but there are many resources on different goddesses available including *365 Goddess* (Harper San Francisco) by Patricia Telesco and *The New Book of Goddesses and Heroines* (Lewellyn Publications) by Patricia Monaghan. Look closely at the stories told about a goddess before you consider her for your dreams. Yemaja (or Yemoja) is the Nigerian goddess of fertility and flowing waters; wonderful for someone seeking bounty in their life's "fishing," but perhaps a bad idea for the almost-due pregnant woman.

> *"Dreams do more than help us understand ourselves better. They help to awaken us to our full identity...Dreams are the original language of the spiritual path."*
>
> —Rosemary Ellen Guiley

The face of the Goddess

Looking into and understanding the face of the Goddess is a strong element of recognizing Her and connecting with Her in your dreams. Meditation can be used to mirror the power of dreaming and show you Her face. The three-day ritual that follows can be performed to intensify the imagery of the Goddess and your connection to Her within your dreams. Over the course of three nights perform the following ritual exactly as prescribed. Do not discuss the outcomes with your Dream Pal or friends until all three nights are complete.

Step 1: Create sacred space in a darkened room.

Step 2: Set up a small mirror so that you can see into it without seeing other items in the room. A single candle that you also cannot see in the mirror should light the room and mirror.

Step 3: Look into the mirror. Let the image of your face fill the surface of the mirror. Continue to focus on the mirror for 15 minutes. Begin by clearing your mind of all preconceived results from this ritual. Imagine only that you are looking into your face, a new face to you, and that you are part of the Goddess. (Hint: It sometimes helps to let your eyes go slightly out of focus.)

Step 4: This ritual takes approximately 15 minutes each night. Use your own internal sense of time, a timer, or some-one outside of the room to signal when your time is up. Re-member to close your ritual space.

Step 5: Record your thoughts, reactions, and any insights in your journal. Do not be discouraged if you do not have significant results on the first two nights. The ritual lasts three nights for a reason!

Step 6: (final night) You have the face and hands of a Goddess. After your mirror time, study your hands for a few moments. These are the hands of a Goddess brought to Earth. Look at the hands. What do they tell you about this Goddess? What Goddess has these hands? What does She *do* with Her-self? (Let these thoughts find their way to your journal as well.)

The results from this ritual are often kept secret to allow each person to experience the depth and intensity of the ritual per-sonally. Once you have completed the ritual, however, it is a good idea to share with your dream partner or friends the imagery and thoughts that appeared during your meditations.

You may find that your face blurred, changed, or metamorphosed into people or animals as your personal energy resonated with the mirror. During the ritual, you were looking into yourself, and the images you saw are alternate images of yourself as a creature of the Goddess. Some people with the gift of prophesy see the past or the future, some people see totem animals and their own face without the masks used in daily life. Still other people find that the ritual is frustrating and there are no images or thoughts that surface. If you were unable to find this alternate face of the Goddess in your meditation, consider setting this exercise aside so that you may try it again later. Personal issues, inner reluctance, fatigue, and pressure to perform or "see something" can all contribute to frustration rather than insights. Be persistent, however, and return to this exercise at another time.

The personal Goddess

Your ritual dreams connect you to the Goddess and remind you of your intimate place in the world. You are a reflection in the well of the Universe, a piece both apart and a part of the creation. You are a form of the Goddess—another face of Her. Within the dream world, meet this Goddess of the Self as you would meet any other new Goddess. Sacred space in waking, sacred space in dreaming—invoke yourself—what 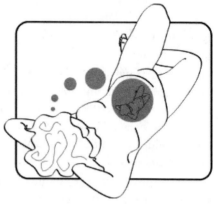 are your characteristics? Your favorite Element? Your "realm" of influence, etc. Answer the same questions posed earlier in this chapter about the Goddess within you. Forget the restrictions of reality because this is your dream and your Goddess. Paint this new Goddess in the best possible light.

Whatever the characteristics of the new Goddess, remember that she is still connected to the pieces of the ancient Mother Goddess that inspired the Willendorf Goddess and countless carvings thousands of years ago. The Willendorf Goddess was faceless, but you have found your personal face for Her and a sacred place to connect with Her in your dreams. The connection you find within your dreams is personal, distinct and powerful beyond the complete understanding of anyone else. Much of this power comes from your belief and faith in this new Goddess—in you. Take refuge in the dream world, take heart and take care to respect the elements that combine in the mystical world of dreams: the Universe, the Self, and the Goddess.

Journal

Dream Pocket

As you explore your relationship with a Goddess, you will discover Her likes and dislikes. The information that you find while reading about a particular Goddess will help you design your own dream pocket. Remember to keep the scents simple and clearly connected to the purpose for your dreams. Look to the Appendix for descriptions of some Goddesses and their favorite things.

For your dream pocket try:

- Brigid: A Brigid's cross of reeds, coal, nails, or a straw dolly.
- Yemaya: Sea salt, small shells, or a touch of ocean water (or simple salt water).
- Bast: Catnip.
- Grandmother Spider: Spider web.
- Freya: Jewelry, especially amber.
- Kali: Skulls, small bones, the color red.
- Crone energy: Holly leaves, sage, dried onion, or lettuce seeds.

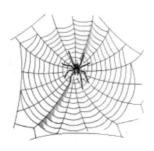

Stepping stones

You have followed a lengthy path in working with your dreams. Imagine you are standing on your path and you can give each stepping stone a name: hope, fear, desire to know. These are the pieces you have put together to lead you down the dreamer's path. Looking at the pathway behind you, what are your reasons for dreaming? What place do dreams have within your life (important advice, moderately important, overwhelming, spiritually helpful on occasion, etc.)? Now look at the steps ahead of you in the distance. What names or labels do your steps in the future have?

Dreams you might not induce

Induced dreams share an important characteristic with more typical or naturally occurring dreams: the missing element is often important. Look carefully at your lucid or induced dreams for pieces that are not included (familiar people, places, experiences, etc.). Make a short list of these topics and reasons why you might not choose to dream of these things. Are these issues that you are not dealing with (as you might if you were overwhelmed) or are you avoiding these topics out of habit? Choose one topic that you are avoiding out of habit (or one that is a few years old) and that you feel you can explore without great distress. Consciously use your sacred dream space (and perhaps the support of your favorite Goddess) to encounter the issues you have been avoiding. Remember that you are in control of the sacred dream space and are safe from harm.

The familiar Goddess

List or identify your favorite goddesses. (Remember, tastes can change over time.) Try to briefly answer the "Getting to know all about you" questions (pages 184-185) for each of these goddesses. Next, select two goddesses that you have heard mentioned briefly and answer the same questions for them. Did you learn new things about familiar goddesses? Did the information about the new goddesses surprise you? Share your findings with your Dream Pal.

Talking time

Now that you have established a connection to your Goddess (old, new, or within), keep up the good work! Work to discover the time period (day of the week, month, or phase of the moon) that works best for your dreaming goddesses. List your favorites and least favorites and the times that dreaming worked well. Mark these times on your calendar so that when you are concerned or want to work on your own growth you can easily find a goddess with a strong connection to that time. Some dreamers use astrological moon phases (the moon passes through the entire Zodiac during its path around the sun) to develop a chart of goddesses, while others use Numerology, divination, or instinct.

Working alone, or with your Dream Pal, set up a series of questions that you can explore over the next six months. Questions could include *Why do I feel spiritually unsettled? Does my spiritual path need to become more community/group oriented? Should I remain a solitary?* Leave a few weeks for each question, because it may take many dreams and a great deal of work to gain an understanding of your answers. List those questions and the time periods below. Make a luncheon or dinner date with your dream partner to discuss the answers and results of your sacred dreaming.

Dictionary of Dream Terminology, Symbols, and Goddesses

This dictionary of symbols is only a helpful sampling of information to inform and inspire you. Use these listings for suggestions when you are working on your dream maps, writing down associations, and especially for exploring the Earth-centered religious symbols within your dreams. Many common dream symbols have been omitted because there are a plethora of dream dictionaries and symbol books that can explain the societal and Universal meanings for an item. The three sections of this dictionary are *Dream Terminology, Symbolism and Imagery*, and *Goddesses*.

Dream Terminology

Alpha waves: Smooth and regular brain waves that are typical of an awake and relaxed person. This type of brain wave activity occurs when a person is in the beginning stages of sleep, but not when they are dreaming.

Astral travel: The time when a soul or spirit is able to travel to distant places or times without taking the physical body. This is most often done on a parallel plane of existence called the *astral plane.*

Beta waves: The regular brain waves of an alert and awake person. These waves can also occur during stress or anxiety. This type of brain wave activity occurs during REM sleep when a person is most likely to be dreaming. This is the same wave pattern of the Earth.

Dream: The collection of images, thoughts, ideas, and feelings that are the product of deep sleep.

Imagery: A set of words or vivid pictures that are used collectively to portray an idea or evoke an emotion.

Nightmares: Dreams that typically have images or concepts that evoke fear, horror, or anxiety in the dreamer.

Prophetic dreams: Dreams which tell about events before they happen. Often these dreams are difficult to verify and represent only possibilities rather than certain fact.

REM: An acronym for rapid eye movement, the condition during the last phase of sleep that coincides with beta waves in the brain and probably dreaming.

Sacred dream space: The spiritual sanctuary created within the dream world through either lucid or induced dreams. This space is a reflection of ritual space created in the sleeping space of the dreamer.

Sleep cycle: The time period required (average is 90 minutes) for a person to move through all of the stages of sleep, including dreaming.

Symbolism: The use of one item within a dream to represent another item or concept.

Symbolism and Imagery

The following symbols are very general and should serve as a starting point for understanding your own dream symbols. The "definitions" are really just ideas and thoughts that are associated with an item that you may or may not have considered. It is a good idea to keep a short dictionary of your own for symbols that recur in your dreams. List symbols, ideas, themes, places, etc. that appear in your dreams on a regular basis and your personal "definition" for these symbols.

Community symbols

This brief list contains symbols from your surroundings, your community. These are most often symbols brought into your dreams by the Universe around you.

Cities: What slogans or names are associated with a city? What strong characteristic do you associate with it? For example, Philadelphia is "the city of brotherly love," while New York "never sleeps." Atlanta can be a symbol of Southern hospitality, technological advancement, and "the Bible belt."

Commercials: Consider the jingles and slogans from commercials. Even commercials that you hate will stay with you. This is a possible symbol for keeping something in your life because it's convenient or because the people around you accept it. The coffee company that used an on-going story line in its commercials successfully kept America looking for the happy romantic ending. Maxwell House's "Good to the last drop" is good, but it is the last drop. Are you being "wrung out" even when you are appreciated?

Pop culture: Singers, television, games, and trends are all likely to appear within your dreams as community symbols. What idea do you associate with the piece of pop culture? For example, Madonna can suggest outrageous clothing and behavior, but she could also represent shrewd business acumen, a successful career, and living life on her own terms, including the job of being a mother. Even punk rockers can symbolize belonging since being part of a sub-culture or counter-culture has become popular.

Shopping malls: These are strongly associated with commercialism, but they have also become the 20th century's answer to a place for people to gather and relax. Malls could represent a feeling of belonging, community, capitalism, and a large variety of choices.

Restaurants: Food has long been associated with happiness, and restaurants are no exception. Feeding the body while gathering with friends is a comfort and often a celebration.

Roads: These modern conveyances suggest the type of path you are traveling or wish to travel. Do you drive down a country road in horse and buggy (old fashioned, reliable)? Super highway in a sedan (main stream)? Are you driving in the fast lane in a DeSoto (right place, right time, wrong tools)?

Personal symbols

Body: References to your own body and its parts often involve your thoughts, feelings, and uses for your body. Hands: Will, intellect, control generally without strength; Feet: Grounding, balance in physical and spiritual worlds, freedom of motion; Face: The Self, perspective on yourself, the eyes particularly can tell you how your inner Self views you (judgmental, open and accepting, curious, etc.).

Childhood toys: At first, these might represent the freedom and fun of youth, but on a deeper level they may also communicate the need to appreciate the simple joys. They might also suggest that you let go and put aside these things from the past.

Family: Aside from their relationship to you in the family, the people around you often play a specific role in your life.

Does your grandmother judge you, your grandfather share special moments? Do you quietly understand and sympathize with a cousin's problems?

Mirrors: While mirrors symbolize a reflection of the Self, they also show you a different perspective of yourself. This is what others see, so look closely. Mirrors in the waking world are non-judgmental and "don't lie," but dream mirrors can show you perspectives other than reality.

Relationships: Whether with friends, family, or coworkers, you interact differently with everyone. A friend brings that friendship, and your feelings about that friendship, into the dream. Often people will subconsciously select friends to balance pieces of their own personality.

Symbols of Earth-centered religions

The following items are associated with Earth-centered or Pagan religions. The symbols that are familiar to Pagans do not normally appear in dream dictionaries. These "definitions" are simply suggested associations and symbols. Your personal understanding of these symbols will always be more powerful and spiritually connected than a generalization. Symbols for the following ideas are listed within the parentheses.

Air: Images of Air appear in dreams to give you the insights offered by the mind, by memory, and to blow away the confusion of difficult situations. (Sky, thought, mental insights, new beginnings, East or North, subtle currents, breath of Life, birds and airplanes, blue or white, feathers.)

Aging: Most Earth-centered religions view aging as natural and older people in the community are seen as wise. (Accelerated aging in a dream is equated to wisdom beyond your time; aging in general indicates a connection to the Cycle of Life or learning lessons with time.)

Altar: A place to arrange the tools for a religious ceremony and a focus for the energy of a ceremony. Altars can represent the overall state of your spiritual life. Orderly but barren might suggest you have not invested your emotions; many tools but dull colors might suggest that you have the knowledge but not the enthusiasm for this kind of spiritual work.

Ancestors: Ancestors are people who are related to you(through blood or through a link with mankind) who have passed from this existence to another. They remind you of bigger issues for humanity rather than just your own issues. (People you know who are deceased, items from other time periods, familiar objects or actions associated with a deceased person.)

Animals (especially as totems): Particularly in native cultures such as the Tslagi (Cherokee) Native Americans, each type of animal has qualities and wisdom (sometimes called "medicine") to lend you in the dream world. (A whale indicates memory or persistence; a coyote is a trickster, but also a teacher of much needed lessons.)

Astrological signs and astrology: The wealth of information and energy that can be presented in your dreams related to astrology is immense. Your understanding of the subject will determine how much astrological symbolism will appear in your dreams. Look carefully at commonly accepted associations for astrological signs, planets, and phases of the moon, but also look at your own associations. For more detail, look to astrology books and resources on the Internet.

During the moon's monthly cycle it moves through the 12 signs of the Zodiac, spending a little more than two days in each sign. There are other factors to consider, but here is a general list of what dreaming in each sign is likely to contain:

- Aries: New beginnings, new understanding, the head.
- Taurus: Relationship to Mother Earth, caretaking of all kinds, determination.

- Gemini: Mirrors, the connection between all things, learning.
- Cancer: Regeneration and procreation, the womb (organ associated with dreaming).
- Leo: Theatres, parties, enjoyment of life, hair, and intelligence.
- Virgo: Order, scientific understanding, intestines, healing dreams.
- Libra: Balance and justice (or lack thereof) on many levels, the kidneys.
- Scorpio: Birth/death/rebirth, profound changes, the nose (aromatherapy).
- Sagittarius: Religious experiences and ceremonies, blood.
- Capricorn: Ancient knowledge, connection to Earth, bones and knees.
- Aquarius: Community, telepathy, tornadoes and tidal waves.
- Pisces: Underwater, secrecy, escape, loyalty, solitude.
- Void-of-course (when the moon is between the influence of these signs for a few hours): These hours do not normally inspire much dreaming, but any dreams that do appear during this time should get your particular attention.

Athame: A ritual knife used in religious ceremonies. Often this knife symbolizes the will and focus of the owner. (A small white or black handled knife, sword, edged weapon of any kind, or even a pair of scissors if the owner is of two minds about something.)

Beaded necklaces: Often called *elekes* by African diaspora religions, the specific associations change with each separate path, but they are generally believed to be a personal connection to the Divine. These could represent your personal connection to the Divine or your desire to understand the African diaspora religions and their power.

Bones: Shared by every human to ever live, these connect you to humanity. Bones also represent the pieces of the Self that we do not often recognize, but that are essential. An archetypal dream of collecting bones and building a new person represents the recreation of your image or your Self. (Animal bones, viewing your bones through your skin.)

Bonfires: Free spirits gather around bonfires to express themselves in drumming, dancing, a deep enjoyment of Life, and each other. Bonfires also represent the primal need for warmth and community; they connect us to ancestors who gathered around fires in times past; and they consume completely but return energy to you. (Flames, beach fires.)

Brooms: Many Pagan religions use brooms to sweep away negative energy, and they might represent a need to cleanse your Life. (Sweeping, vacuuming, household brooms.)

Candles: Candles are used to focus specific energy depending on the size, color, and placement of the candle. Symbolically, candles are consumed, but their energy is evident as light and warmth. Candlelight is often most flattering to rough images or situations. (Hope is represented by a lit candle; endings are represented by an extinguished candle.)

Centering: A process of removing outside distractions and being present in the moment. (You need centering in a dream if there is dizziness or disorienting carnival rides; visually placing a project in the middle of a page; or placing things around you at equal distances.)

Chalice (cup): The female or receptive aspect of humanity; the womb; creation. Combined with the athame (knife), they represent the Cycle of Life and completion. If you are in a religious setting within a dream, do these items appear together? (Coffee cups, wine glasses, drinking vessels of all kinds.)

Children: These little people are the beginning of the Cycle of Life and are often used within dreams to represent the youth of mankind, the past, or your own youth. Memories surface in dreams when they can reflect on or add insight into a current situation.

Circles: Perfection; completion; safety; the completion of Nature's Cycle of Life; the wholeness of the Universe; the perfection of Life as it is; the path of the soul as it moves through the world. While circles appear in everyday life, look closely at unusually formed circles (flowers in the grass and the faery circle) or round objects that catch your attention in a dream.

Earth: Body of the Goddess; Mother Earth; beginning and ending point of your body; the womb of the Universe; a resting point and place of stillness. The Earth appears in dreams as a stable touchstone, a beginning point for the next step. Plant your feet firmly, but not permanently, because even Mother Earth changes over time. (The colors brown or green, undines or gnomes, caves, mountains, streams.)

Elements: The basic pieces of all Life represent strong power without needs or direction. Whether you use the four American Elements (Earth, Air, Fire, Water), the Oriental Elements (Earth, Metal, Wood, Water, Air), or the three Celtic Realms (Earth, Air, Water) you are still using basic building blocks. (See each Element individually for correspondences.)

Fire: Strong energy; passion; purification; creativity. Fire appears in a dream to suggest consuming changes, new forms (wood to ash, metal to be formed into swords) and the light that covers everything. (The color red, blood, salamanders, sun and stars, flames, matches.)

Herbs: These plant medicines represent cures that work without understanding; Nature's healing; and the balance of Nature. While individual herbs may have their own significance, overall, herbs appear within dreams as a spice to add flavor to your dream or as a tool for healing. For specifics, consult a good herbal handbook such as Patricia Telesco's *The Herbal Arts* (Citadel Press).

Initiation: Desire for progress; inward change being recognized; connection with power that is already there; spiritual growth. Initiations within dreams can be an indication that you will receive lessons and grow spiritually. They are also used to remind you to acknowledge inner changes to yourself. (Rituals, passageways, doors, obstacles.)

Moon phases: The phases of the moon represent natural variation over time; the Cycle of Life; the undeniable pull of the Universe (most often seen as the sea, the tides, or the seasons). The moon appears in dreams to remind you of the feminine, the Goddess in all Her aspects (phases of the moon), and the special connection women have to the creative power of the Universe. Note the phase of the moon. New moons are for beginnings and an increase in energy. Waxing crescent moons symbolize growth, increasing bounty, and things coming to (but not yet at) fruition. Full moon indicates maturity, something coming to fullness. Waning moons are the passing away of old ideas, fading of negative energy, and declining age. (Moon, the colors silver or white, circles.)

Nudity: The naked body suggests social taboos; physicality; basic human needs and desires; removing obstacles and restrictions. While modern society has clothed the human body in degrading needs, Earth-centered religions tend to view the body as a piece of the world to be honored and cared for, even as you would care for a temple. Often your body will appear nude as a way of pointing out your inhibitions and your need for protection. (Dolls without clothes, your own or others' nudity.)

Numbers: Numerology is the study of numbers to gain meaning and insight into the world around you. Numbers with specific spiritual importance appear in nearly every culture, most often these are prime numbers: 1, 3, 5, and 7. They symbolize specific things within each path, but generally they connect with time, counting, limits, and patterns within Nature. (Clocks, numbers of items, etc.)

Offerings: These are items placed before or on an altar so that the energy of the item can be "given" to the Goddess. Offerings represent a willing acknowledgement; giving of oneself; sacrifice; or supplication. The offering is given with the intention of gaining a blessing, a favor or the attention of a Divine power. Offerings might appear in your dreams as a suggestion that one is needed, or as a reminder that you must sacrifice or lose something valuable in order to gain your goal. (Lent, denied food, symbolic representations of animals or actions.)

Persecution/Inquisition: Modern-day Witches have a strong connection to the history of magick. The Spanish Inquisition and the trials in Salem, Massachusetts were terrifying events, but they can live on in your dreams as images from the past. (Being burned alive, floating in a river, being pressed or hung.)

Shamans: These medicine men represent a connection with the Earth around them and the unknown world of spirits; the need to scavenge for tools in every situation; mysterious medicine; altered states of consciousness to connect with the Divine. Shamans often appear in dreams to encourage you to walk your own path, listen to your instincts, and to use the elements at hand rather than seeking formal tools. (Eyes with large pupils, "wild" looking men, rattles.)

Spirit: This is sometimes called the fifth and final Element of the natural Elements and it likely represents purity and spirituality. (The color white, doves, stars, angels, heart chakra.)

Tarot: Tarot, as well as other forms of divination, often appear as you are trying to determine the outcome of a situation or your next step. Tarot symbols, in general, represent divination, seeking answers, intuition, and deep symbolism. (Cups, swords, rods, coins.)

Threefold Law: The idea that your actions come back to you three times over. This law also suggests a personal responsibility to the dreamer. (Meeting people in threes, the triple Goddess, house numbers.)

Water: Water appears in dreams as a touchstone for emotions, slow changes, and the womb. (Fish, the colors blue and deep sea green, seashells, waterfalls, rivers, tears.)

Witch: Society has developed a stereotype of Witches that uses some standard elements (Female, old, ugly, broom, black hat and cat, etc.). Perhaps the black dress isn't just to look slim at the party, but represents your subconscious "announcement" that you fall into that category known by most people as "a Witch."

Goddesses

Artemis: This Greek virginal moon Goddess personifies Natural law. She is a complex Goddess who represents the many possibilities of womanhood. She seems contradictory because She is a virgin who promotes promiscuity, rules hunting (as an archer) while protecting animals, and protects women in childbirth while bringing death and sickness. (Arrows, animals, forests.)

Asase Yaa: West African Goddess also known as "Old Woman Earth" who rules fertility. She is the ancestral mother who gave birth to humanity and reclaims them at death. She gave cultivation to humans. (Earth-toned colors, Thursday.)

Astarte (also known as Ishtar or Anunitu): This Egyptian Goddess ruled sexuality as a wanton with wild woman energy.

She was depicted as a warrior Goddess robed in flames and "armed with a sword and two quivers full of death-dealing arrows." (Red and white colors, the acacia tree, cypress, horses, firstborn children.)

Baba Yaga (also Baba Iaga): Lithuanian/Russian Goddess or Witch of regeneration, she is an archetypal Crone who rules over birds and beasts; day and night respond to her call. She traveled in a mortar with a pestle as a paddle. She lives in a hut that stands upon chicken legs in the deep forest surrounded by a fence of bones. (Corn sheaves, wreaths of grains, and wildflowers.)

Bast (also Bastet): Egyptian Goddess with the head of a lion or cat. She rules music, dance, animals, magick, the power to overcome, playfulness, joy, and humor. (Cats, cat eyes, sunset, month of May.)

Braciaca: She is a Gaulish agricultural Goddess who includes in Her realms brewers, Nature, abundance and harvest, dreams, summer, and fall. (Grapes, vines, wine, grape juice.)

Brigid: This famous Celtic triple Goddess rules goldsmithing, scholarship, poetry, arcane lore, divination and prophecy, and she protects women in childbirth. She has two sisters who are associated with healing and crafts. She brought whistling and keening (Irish mourning) to humans. (February 1st, Brigid's cross of reeds, cauldron, anvil, triscales, fire, brass shoes.)

Brizo: This Greek Goddess of the sea protected ships and crews. She was also a prophet and specialist in dream interpretation. (Boats, waves, dreamers.)

Cerridwen: Sometimes known as "the Witch's Witch," Cerridwen is a Welsh Mother Goddess linked closely with the moon and lunar powers, fertility, creativity, the harvest, inspiration, knowledge, and luck. Through a series of trials, she gave birth to the poet Taliesin. (Cauldron, pig, grain, stereo-typical "witchy" things.)

Coatlicue: This Aztec Earth Goddess rules the moon, creation, and the end of life. While still a virgin she became pregnant (from jade stones or emeralds) and gave birth to the god Quetzalcoatl. After his birth she entered a misty world where no one recognized her magnificence. (Jade, emeralds, snakes, claws.)

Danu: As an ancestor of the Tuatha De Danann (People of Danu), this Irish Mother Goddess represents wisdom. Her name derives from the ancient Celtic word meaning "knowledge."

Daphne: Although she is not a Goddess, this priestess called out to Mother Earth while being pursued by the Sun God and she became a laurel tree. She is the guardian who gives women escape from sexual transgression; inspiration; women's power; and rituals. (Laurel tree, nudity.)

Demeter: This strong Greek Mother Goddess ruled over crops (especially grains) and the fertility of the land and the women. As the grieving mother of Persephone, she wandered the Earth wearing a blue-green cloak that was shredded like cornflowers in the grass. Offerings to her are made in their natural state (honeycombs, wool, grapes, grain) and not consumed in fires. (Mirror, grains, cornflowers, blue or green.)

Diana: Fertility, children, abundance, the open sky, and the harvest are the realms protected by this Roman Goddess. Aside from one priest, she was worshipped almost entirely by women. (Cornucopia, clouds, sky, blue, August 15th.)

Fortuna: This Goddess rules fate, wealth, luck, abundance, and destiny. (Wheel, cornucopia.)

Freya: A Nordic Goddess of devotion, strength, sun, magick, passion, sexuality, and sexual freedom, she is also a ruler of love and the heart. She is sometimes pictured riding a chariot pulled by cats, in the form of a bird, or a woman with a feathered cloak. She cries tears of gold. (Lion, strawberries, sunshine, birds, cats, linen.)

Hecate: This Greco-Roman Goddess is sometimes used as the archetypal Crone figure. She rules fate, opportunities, sorcery, the moon, beginnings, ritual purification, invocations, and magick. She is most often pictured at crossroads and accompanied by the mournful baying of hounds. She was sometimes seen as the dark of the moon, with Artemis ruling the waxing moon and Selene ruling the full moon. (Serpent, horse or dog, lighted torches, myrrh, silver and moonstone, honey.)

Hina: Tahitian Goddess ruling the moon, communication, natural cycles, death, and meditation. As she changes with the moon she rules different aspects that reflect the full life cycle of women. She is a woman who grew the first coconut and possibly the warrior of the Island of Women. (Anything associated with the moon, white, silver, and coconut.)

Iduna: Teutonic Goddess ruling love, divination, dreams, and longevity. She was born of flowers and protects the apples of immortality. (Apples and flowers.)

Ishtar (also known as Inanna): This Babylonian Goddess is known to have the energy of a wild woman and a wanton. She rules love, fertility, passion, sexuality, the fullness of womanhood, nurturing, and the moon. She is thought to be the morning star, the evening star, or the moon. Also called the "Lady of battles," Inanna descended into the Underworld through seven gates to try to take over, but she failed. (Star, the number seven, moon, lion, dove.)

Isis: This Egyptian Goddess is a devoted wife and mother who rules over weaving, spinning, sorcery, magick, harvest, dreams, divination, perspective, faithfulness, oracular insight, inner beauty, love, spirituality, and destiny. She is revered as the Goddess who taught humans the basic skills for civilization and she invented the process of embalming. (Bloodstone, amethyst, myrrh, cedar, hawk, moon and its associated colors of white and silver.)

Ix Chel: Mayan Goddess living in the land of mists and rainbows. Ix Chel rules weather, children, weaving, medicine, fertility, and health. She wears a skirt of fertile waters with water lilies, but sometimes she is depicted as an old woman with serpents in her hair, and with the eyes and claws of a jaguar. Her lover was jealous and she left him to wander the night as she wished. She is a wonderful goddess for the independence in every woman. (Water, turquoise, jade, silver, blue or white items, dragonflies, water lilies.)

Kali: This Hindu Goddess of birth and rebirth, cycles, dance, creation, destruction, joy, courage, cleansing, and change is often perceived as a dark goddess. She reminds you that out of negative situations you can "rebirth" new ideas and beginnings. Kali is dark-skinned, emaciated, and wears a tiger skin and a necklace of skulls. She offers her followers the chance to face their fears and becomes a comforting mother to those who do. (Flowers, dance, iron, sword, peacock feathers, honey.)

Kore: This archetypal maiden is the Greek Goddess of luck, cycles, and youthful energy. (Coins, corn, 7, flower buds, pomegranate)

Kwan Yin: She is the Chinese Goddess of peace, wealth, protector of children and all people in distress, kindness, magick, health, and fertility. She is the ideal mother who gives freely of her unending sympathy and magickal insight, if asked. She encourages enlightenment and hears every prayer of the world. Her followers eat no flesh and inflict no violence on other beings. (Lotus, black tea, willows, rice, rainbow.)

Maat: Egyptian Goddess who rules the aspects of freedom, new beginnings, truth, justice, morality, organization, promises, and divine order. (Feathers of any kind, especially ostrich.)

Nina: This ancient Mesopotamian Mother Goddess rules health, cooperation, dreams, magick, and mediation. She helped civilization along when it was needed. (Lions, fish, serpent.)

Nisaba: A Sumerian Goddess, Nisaba rules creativity, communication, excellence, inspiration, Universal law, divination, and dreams. She invented literacy, encouraged creativity, and brought astrology and architecture to mankind. Dream interpretation (because of her creativity and literacy) was a particular gift for Nisaba. (Pens, computers, books, snakes.)

Oya: As the spirit of the river Niger, this Yoruban mother Goddess rules the areas of justice, memory, tradition, zeal, and femininity. She is a warrior Goddess with wild woman energy, as well as patron of female leadership. She is also a Goddess who can control ghosts. (Water, Fire, the number nine, buffalo horns.)

Selene: This Greek Goddess of the moon put her lover into a magick sleep to keep him young forever. She is sometimes pictured with wings, crowned with a crescent, and driving a lunar chariot across the sky. (Wings, infinity symbol, youthfulness, moon.)

Tara: This Hindu Goddess was a mediator who included wisdom, Universal unity, peace, Self-mastery, mysticism, cooperation, destiny, energy, and spirituality in Her realms. She encompasses all time and the spark of Life and extends to us to fill our spiritual hunger. (Star, sparks of flame.)

Valkeries: These shapeshifting Germanic Goddesses rule fate, destiny, and weaving. These are protective spirits that are often depicted as female mounted warriors. (Ravens, blood, 9.)

Wawilak Sisters: These Australian heroines of the Dreamtime reportedly shaped the environment and named everything as they journeyed across the primordial landscape. (Variety of animal forms and trees.)

White Shell Woman: This Native American Goddess (or spirit) brought the gifts of dreams, shamanism, the Elements, sunshine for protection, and renewed hope. It is said that a rainbow banished all sadness after her arrival. (Eagle, rattle, dreams, rainbows.)

Ymoja (Yemaja): This Nigerian Mother Goddess of flowing water rules over blessings, luck, and fertility. She is sometimes seen as a Goddess of the sea. As Yemaya Olokun she is so powerful that she can only be seen in dreams. (Fish, the color blue, the crescent moon, mermaids.)

Bibliography

Blair, Nancy. *Goddesses for Every Season*. Rockport, Mass.: Element Books, Inc., 1995.

Carroll, William. *Superstitions 10,000 You Really Need*. San Marcos, Calif.: Coda Publications, 1998.

Cunningham, Scott. *Dreaming the Divine: Techniques for Sacred Sleep*. St. Paul, Minn.: Llewellyn Publications, 1999.

———. *Sacred Sleep: Dreams and the Divine*. Freedom, Calif.: The Crossing Press, 1992.

Estes, Clarissa Pinkola, Ph.D. *Women Who Run With The Wolves*. New York, N.Y.: Ballantine Books, 1997.

Gelb, Michael J. *How to Think Like Leonardo da Vinci: Seven Steps to Genius Every Day*. New York, N.Y.: Delacorte Press, 1998.

Guiley, Rosemary Ellen. *Dreamwork for the Soul: A Spiritual Guide to Dream Interpretation*. New York, N.Y.: Berkley Books, 1998.

Hagan, Kay Leigh. *Internal Affairs : A journalkeeping workbook for self-intimacy*. Atlanta, Ga.: Escapadia Press, 1988.

Koch-Sheras Ph.D., Phyllis R and Peter L. Sheras. *The Dream Sharing Sourcebook*. Los Angeles, Calif.: RGA Publishing Group.

Miller, Gustavus Hindman. *10,000 Dreams Interpreted: An Illustrated Guide to Unlocking the Secrets of Your Dreamlife.* Element Books Limited, 1996. Text Revised Barnes & Noble, 1996.

Monaghan, Patricia. *The New Book of Goddesses & Heroines* 3rd ed. St. Paul, Minn. Llewellyn Publications, 1981.

Parker, Julia & Derek. *The Complete Book of Dreams.* DK Publishing, Inc., 1995.

Sams, Jamie. *Dancing the Dream: The Seven Sacred Paths of Human Transformation.* San Francisco, Calif.: Harper Collins Publishers, 1999.

Sun Bear and Wabun Wind. *Dreaming with the Wheel.* New York, N.Y.: Simon & Schuster, Inc., 1994.

Telesco, Patricia. *365 Goddess: A Daily Guide to the Magic and Inspiration of the Goddess.* San Francisco, Calif.: HarperCollins Publishers, 1998.

————. *A Victorian Grimoire.* St. Paul, Minn.: Llewellyn Publications, 1992.

————. *The Language of Dreams.* Freedom, Calif.: The Crossing Press, 1997.

Vedfelt, Ole. *The Dimensions of Dreams, from Freud and Jung to Boss, Perls and R.E.M.: A Comprehensive Sourcebook.* New York, N.Y.: International Publishing Co.

Web Resources

www.journalforyou.com

www.Dreamtree.com

www.dreamloverinc.com

www.au-naturel.net

members.aol.com/aarenka/lucidintro.html

Index

About the Author

Scarlett Ross is constantly amazed at the places her path has led her, but she has not wandered far from her birthplace in Atlanta, Georgia. Her husband, young son, and two cats share her home. She was formally educated in public schools during the school year and informally educated in the rural counties of Georgia during the summers. After graduating from Oglethorpe University, she began teaching high school English in an alternative program. After her son was born she was given the opportunity to stay at home and pursue her dream of sharing through written works.

Dreams of the Goddess is the first full-length result of her new career and it is the culmination of years of dreaming. It was the need to find answers for her dreams that guided her toward the metaphysical and Pagan paths. She has wandered through libraries of books, hours of discussion, and years of training in her search for the meaning in her dreams. What she found eventually gave meaning to her dreams but the teacher within wasn't satisfied. She needed a way to blend her desire to teach and her personal spiritual search on dreams— and then she was offered the opportunity to write this book.

Ms. Ross considers herself a Southern Celtic Shamanistic Kitchen Witch. The Southern grace and hospitality are part of her modern heritage just as the Celtic and Native American shaman practices are part of her ancient heritage. Ultimately, though, she is the ever practical, ever cooking Kitchen Witch with flavors from the past and present. Her spiritual teachers have included Wiccans, Gardnerians, radicals, Native Americans, and shamans. Her training includes study with groups, work with individual teachers, and periods of time as a solitary practitioner.

Her current projects include a series of workshops on personal divinity; workshops and retreats on women's spirituality; dreaming; and writing. These workshops have been strongly inspired by her transitional experiences and meditations. Often her meditations and insights are influenced by what it means to be female and to connect the Goddess.

Children, especially, hold an honored place in her life. Although she retired from teaching in public school a few years ago, she continues to work with her own child and with the youth of the Pagan community. When she is not writing, she is directing a summer camp program for Indigo Village, a non-profit holistic educational organization dedicated to helping the entire child develop on all levels—mental, physical, creative, spiritual, etc. Beyond these short-term projects she continues to develop plans and lay the groundwork for ShadowBrook, a retreat and education center to serve the Pagan and metaphysical communities.